KOSHER COOKBOOK
FOR THE FAMILY

D1601803

KOSHER COOKBOOK

FOR THE FAMILY

75 RECIPES TO MAKE AT HOME

JAMIE FEIT, MS, RD

PHOTOGRAPHY BY DARREN MUIR

ROCKRIDGE PRESS

CONTENTS

INTRODUCTION

Growing up, so much of my family life was defined by food. On weekends, as soon as we finished breakfast, my mother was already discussing what to make for lunch. I grew up in a Jewish household, and although we didn't keep kosher, my mother made many traditional Jewish recipes—many passed down to her from my grandmother. Once I got married, she passed down those recipes and cooking skills to me, and I still use those recipes today. In fact, two of my favorite recipes in this book come straight from my grandmother (see Grandma Dotty's Brisket, page 82, and Grandma Dotty's Brownies, page 109), and I think of her every time I prepare them.

My kosher journey began when I got married. My husband was raised in a kosher household, and once we married, we agreed we would keep kosher as well. Since I was new to it, I had lots of questions, and I found answers through books like *Spice and Spirit: The Complete Kosher Jewish Cookbook* and *Fast & Festive Meals for the Jewish Holidays*. I also got advice from my husband's family, our rabbi, and so many members of our community.

I quickly learned that kosher food is much more than the traditional Jewish foods I grew up eating. Some kosher rules were easy to learn: Avoid pork and shellfish, and only purchase kosher meat and cheese. Others took more getting used to, like separating milk and meat (and organizing the kitchen to keep them separate). With practice, I was able to master delicious kosher recipes that still provided the depth of flavor I was used to. In this book, I'll show you how to do just this.

All of the recipes in this book have been tested on my husband and four teenage daughters—my biggest helpers and my most prominent critics. I'm always teaching them how to prepare delicious kosher meals, and I hope the knowledge and love I put into my cooking will resonate with them so that they, too, pass these recipes on to the next generation.

Jewish tradition and food are inexorably intertwined. (Ask anyone who's cooked a Shabbat lunch—many of us cook more food for this one weekly meal than most people make for Thanksgiving!) It's like a holiday every week, and that doesn't even account for actual holiday meals, like Rosh Hashanah and Passover. Doing so much cooking can be tiring, but it's always worth the work and can be quite gratifying. After all, food is part of how we share and preserve our commitment to Judaism, keeping our traditions over thousands of years.

This book includes plenty of quick and easy weekday recipes as well as some challenging Shabbat and holiday recipes. I hope the traditional recipes evoke some good old-fashioned nostalgia, and I hope the simple ones help you feel prepared to keep a kosher kitchen even when you're short on time. I've also included plenty of modern, healthy recipes that reflect my 20-plus years of professional training as a nutritionist—it was and is important to me to prepare healthy and delicious food, and I've learned so many incredible ways to combine keeping kosher with eating healthy.

Over the years, I've prepared more delicious, memorable kosher meals than I can count. I'd venture to say I have somewhat of a reputation as a go-to person for mouthwatering, healthy, and enjoyable food that everyone will enjoy. I hope the recipes in this book help you share meals with your family and community for years to come. My secrets to an abundant kosher kitchen are yours—bring an appetite!

CHAPTER 1

What Does It Mean to Keep Kosher at Home?

Keeping kosher at home can seem intimidating at first glance, but it's completely manageable and so rewarding. Food brings people together: It allows us to pass down our family traditions and make new memories. As a nutritionist, my goal is to help people prepare delicious, healthy food. I firmly believe that to be truly healthy, you must make room in your life for happiness and joy, through family, community, and shared experiences.

That's where keeping kosher comes in: It guides us in creating meals that connect us to Judaism and uses food as a means for celebration. This is never truer than on Shabbat, when we prepare three meals to enjoy while resting, honoring tradition, and spending time together.

Whether you're new to keeping a kosher home or you're looking for fresh ideas and inspiration, you've come to the right place. This book will go over the nuts and bolts of how to keep kosher in today's world. Chapter 1 focuses on the historical, cultural, and religious aspects of keeping kosher, and the subsequent chapters contain recipes, ranging from traditional dishes to everyday staples to modern adaptations to tried-and-true favorites.

Kashrut Law: All the Food That's Fit to Eat

The history of the Laws of Kashrut begins in the Torah, more than 3,000 years ago to be specific (The Stone Edition of the Chumash, Leviticus 11:1–47 and Deuteronomy 14:3–28). *Kashrut* translates to "fit," meaning food that is fit to be eaten. Kashrut, more commonly described as "kosher," refers to the Jewish dietary laws as laid out in the Torah. Kosher observance has been passed down over generations in Jewish communities around the world.

Kosher dietary patterns vary among the many sects of Judaism. For example, a "kosher-style" household falls on the more casual side: You might exclude pork and shellfish and avoid mixing milk and meat outright, but you might not buy specifically kosher-labeled meat, cheese, or other foods. You may or may not have two sets of dishes for meat and dairy. Some people might follow kosher law at home but eat nonkosher foods at friends' houses or restaurants.

How and when you decide to observe kosher laws is a personal choice. Whether you are glatt kosher, strictly kosher, only kosher in your home, kosher-style, or keep partially kosher for health reasons, the recipes in this book will work for you. They can be used across the spectrum of adherence to kosher law. I practice Modern Orthodox Judaism, and I prepare all this food in my home.

All in all, following the Laws of Kashrut should help connect our food to our religion in a day-to-day sense. As Rabbi Ruth Sohn once wrote, "Kashrut reminds us again and again that Jewish spirituality is inseparable from the physical." Rather than a set of scientific dietary guidelines, kashrut offers structure in the way we eat and helps us carry traditions from generation to generation. I hope this book helps you see just how you can find harmony and joy in keeping kosher, practicing Judaism, and carrying on tradition in the modern age.

The Hows and Whys of Kashrut

As discussed in the previous section, kosher law is laid out as a set of guidelines in the Torah. In this way, consuming food becomes holy, and is intrinsically tied to our religious practice. Kosher food also serves as a focus of nearly every holiday—including Shabbat, which centers around three meals. For example, in Modern Orthodox Judaism (which I practice), we are required to say a blessing over each type of food when we eat it (The Stone Edition of the Chumash, Deuteronomy 8:10). Although communities have unique traditions, cuisines, and specific practices, the kosher laws as written in the Torah remain the same.

There are several passages in the Torah that outline what food may be consumed and how to consume it. Here are the basics of different kosher foods:

Meat and dairy must be separated: At three different points, the Torah instructs us not to "boil a kid in its mother's milk" (The Stone Edition of the Chumash, Deuteronomy 14:21, Exodus 23:19, and Exodus 34:26). Over many generations, this has been interpreted to mean that we must not consume meat and dairy together. There are also varying interpretations about how long to wait between eating meat and then dairy.

Foods may not contain any blood: The Torah states that the life or soul of the animal exists within its blood. Kosher meat must be slaughtered in a specific, humane way to ensure that there is minimal blood and that the animal feels the least pain. The meat is then soaked and salted to drain any blood.

Meat: Consume only animals that have split hooves and chew their cud, such as beef, lamb, and veal. The Torah states specifically that pigs do not fit into this classification—this is why pork (including bacon) may not be consumed. You can read more about kosher butchering in Kosher Cuts: Get to Know Your Butcher (page 14).

Poultry: The poultry prohibited by the Torah are all birds of prey and scavenging birds, but the Torah does not state that these characteristics are the reason for prohibition. All allowed poultry is inferred from these prohibitions.

Dairy: Consume only dairy products that come from a kosher animal and do not use animal flesh. For instance, dairy products made with animal rennet, like some cheeses, are not kosher.

Fish: Consume only fish that have both fins and scales. Shellfish do not fit into this category, so they are not allowed. Swordfish and sturgeon are also prohibited because they lose their scales over time.

Grains, Vegetables, and Fruits: Grains, vegetables, and fruits are considered kosher but must not have insects in or on them. It is common practice to make sure these foods are properly washed. In some Orthodox communities, rabbis have deemed that certain difficult-to-clean fruits and vegetables require special washing to be considered kosher.

Eggs: Eggs must come from a kosher animal, and they must be checked for blood spots (per the above rule). If a spot of blood is found, the egg is not kosher and cannot be eaten.

Pareve foods: The word *pareve* means "neutral" in Yiddish and is a term used for foods that contain neither dairy nor meat. Eggs, fish, fruit, vegetables, and grains are all pareve and can be eaten, prepared, or served with either meat or dairy. Fish is pareve because it is not considered meat or dairy, and while it can be consumed at the same meal as meat, it cannot be served on the same plate. (During meat meals, it's commonly served on a separate plate with different utensils, most often as an appetizer.)

The Culture of Kosher

Given that kosher law is thousands of years old, it has evolved over time to be adapted into countless forms. The basics remain the same as they were laid out many years ago, but since kosher law comes from the Torah, the specific rules are not always spelled out clearly. Over time, questions and debates have arisen as ancient kosher law comes face to face with modernization. As the culture evolves, kosher law continues to evolve with it.

Being kosher is fluid, and people tend to observe kashrut according to what works for their family or what's common in their community. The kosher food industry has also evolved into a multibillion-dollar industry. Some people eat kosher food because they feel it's healthier or that kosher food may be "cleaner" than nonkosher food. Many people who don't actually keep kosher purchase kosher meat because they feel the animals are treated more humanely, especially given modern-day animal slaughterhouse conditions.

In fact, modern knowledge about food safety is sometimes retroactively applied to the rationale behind kosher law. For instance, a common misconception is that pork and shellfish are not kosher because they are considered "unhealthy" or "dirty." This is not the case, and in fact, there is no known scientific basis for kosher law. The reason Jews avoid certain animals is because God commanded the Jewish people to eat only food sanctified as kosher in the Torah.

With that said, in recent decades some Jewish groups have concluded that kosher laws were based on historical health issues that no longer exist in the modern world. This is where some variations of "kosher-style" practice developed, wherein people may eat food that culturally follows kosher designations but is not formally kosher.

As traditions have evolved and morphed over time, debates have emerged on the "proper" ways to keep kosher. One major debate is how long one must wait after eating meat before consuming dairy. Customs range from waiting one hour to three hours to six hours. Other debates have emerged in the wake of relatively modern knowledge—for example, whether fish that shed their scales are still to be considered kosher, or whether animals that are predators are automatically nonkosher.

Again, keeping kosher can come in many forms. I grew up in a Reform Jewish family, and we ate kosher-style food at home only on Friday nights (the beginning of the Sabbath) and Passover. My parents felt keeping this loose interpretation of kashrut helped provide structure for our Jewish home and connected us to my grandparents. We didn't question it—we just adopted and adapted tradition. We didn't buy kosher meat, but we did avoid mixing milk and meat (and eating shellfish) on Friday nights. During Passover, we omitted bread and other leavened foods (eating matzoh instead), and we avoided eating in nonkosher restaurants. It was a lax form of keeping kosher, but it still tied us to tradition.

When I married my husband, we chose to follow Modern Orthodox Judaism and raise our children in this tradition. We follow the Laws of Kashrut, observe Shabbat, and keep a fully kosher kitchen and home. But even within the orthodox communities—which run the gamut from Chasidic to Modern Orthodox and many others in between—kashrut observance varies. Some eat only in glatt kosher restaurants; others will eat dairy at nonkosher restaurants, reasoning that the most stringent prohibitions relate to eating kosher meat and avoiding shellfish.

To say there is a diverse spectrum of kosher observance would be an understatement. Whether you follow the strictest version of kosher law or lean more toward the flexible side, I hope you'll use kosher law as a way to celebrate food and pass down Jewish tradition to the next generation.

A TALE OF TWO KITCHENS

As mentioned on page 3, in keeping kosher, we must not consume dairy with meat. The practical implications of this as kosher law are that we must find ways to keep dairy and meat separate in our kitchens.

In an ideal world, we would have separate kitchens for milk and meat preparation, along with two sets of plates, two sinks, two dishwashers, two ovens, and two microwaves. Restaurants, hotels, and other businesses with kosher kitchens actually do this, but it's not usually practical for home cooking. Most of us don't have access to more than one kitchen, and even more of us are low on kitchen space to begin with.

Working with a single kitchen, our goal should be to prevent cross-contamination and mixing of meat and milk. To do this, Jews who keep kosher have two sets of dishes and basic cookware for milk and meat—this is a basic necessity for a kosher kitchen. (Some people have a full extra set of pareve cookware as well.) When it comes to larger appliances, be practical—you really don't need two of everything to make do. I'll get into more specifics in Seeing Double on page 8.

Keeping a kosher kitchen takes some work (and, if you're new to it, some getting used to), but it's a wonderful way to connect your faith to your everyday life and values. Following the Laws of Kashrut has given me a sense of stability and grounds me in my Jewish identity. I hope this book helps you strengthen your connections to tradition through everyday cooking.

Keeping a Kosher Kitchen

You should set up your kosher kitchen with the following principles in mind:

- Do not keep any nonkosher items in the kitchen.
- Prepare all food using only kosher ingredients.
- Meat and dairy must be prepared, cooked, and served separately.
- Keep separate sets of kitchenware for cooking and serving meat and dairy.

Without a doubt, the most noticeable difference between a regular kitchen and a kosher kitchen is the double sets of cookware. If you don't have two each of your larger appliances, don't fret—you're still completely equipped to keep a kosher kitchen. These next few pages will guide you through it.

Keeping Kosher Cookware

Ideally, a kosher kitchen is set up with two different counters, one dedicated to meat and one to dairy. A few things are essential, such as having two sets of cooking utensils, pots, plates, cutlery, dish drainers/sink liners (or a double-sided sink), and cleaning brushes.

We'll also discuss the process of "koshering" pots, pans, and other kitchen tools that have been used with nonkosher foods so they can be used for kosher cooking (see Kashering, page 10). Here are my essential tips to make keeping kosher cookware easy:

Divide and designate cabinets for both meat and dairy. If you have counter space on both sides of your kitchen, I recommend designating one side for meat and the other side for dairy.

Choose a cabinet for pareve dishware. You don't need a whole counter or pantry for it—you'll just use it to store glassware and/or pareve utensils.

Mark the cabinets with kosher stickers. These stickers come with meat, dairy, and pareve labels and will be immensely helpful in ensuring everyone knows what belongs in which cabinet.

Store large, bulky items in square wicker storage baskets. Get one that matches your kitchen and use it to stack large cooking items like baking sheets, muffin tins, cooling racks, broiling pans, etc. This keeps cabinets clutter-free, and the items will be easy to access.

Invest in a spice rack. This tip isn't specific to kosher kitchens, but keeping bottled spices easily accessible will save you a ton of time when cooking.

Seeing Double

In an ideal world, it would be amazing to have duplicates of every piece of kitchenware. If you do have space to store duplicates of everything, count yourself one of the lucky ones! Most of us don't have that kind of room, but it's still very possible to keep your kitchen kosher. Let me break down which items are essential.

Dishware and cutlery: Ceramic and porcelain dishware is porous and can retain flavors, so you'll need two sets. You'll also need two sets of cutlery, serving utensils, and serving dishes. It's possible to get by with only one set of glassware—since glass is nonporous, it won't absorb any food or flavors, so it can be used for either meat or dairy.

Kitchen tools: You'll need two sets of commonly used cooking utensils, pots and pans, and cutting boards, as well as items like liquid and dry measuring cups, baking sheets and pans, muffin tins, and colanders.

Appliances: Make decisions about expensive or single-use appliances—such as food processors, slow cookers, toasters, and blenders—based on what you cook most often. If you're short on space, I recommend using a food processor for meat, an upright blender for dairy, and two immersion blenders, one for meat and one for dairy. If you plan to use your microwave for both meat and dairy, make sure the food is always tightly covered.

Oven, dishwasher, and sink: These large appliances are the most difficult to find in duplicate, but you can certainly work with what you have. If you don't have two ovens, you'll need to kasher it between baking uncovered meat and dairy dishes (see Kashering, page 10). If you have a dishwasher, you can designate it to be used for either milk or meat, and handwash the other dishes. If you have one sink, use two separate sink drainers for meat and dairy so the dishes don't touch the surface of the sink basin. If you have a double-sided sink with two sink basins, you can use one side for meat and the other side for dairy (and wash pareve dishes on whichever side they were prepared with).

Dining: When splitting your kitchen between meat and dairy, you'll also need to think about where you'll eat. Decide whether your dining table will be used for dairy or meat. If you use it for meat meals, you should use a tablecloth or other covering for dairy meals. You can also use separate sets of meat and dairy placemats.

Good Kitchen Gadgets

Having a few kitchenware basics will make cooking a lot easier, saving you time and making the process so much more enjoyable. Here is my list of essentials—I've indicated when you'll need two sets versus one for meat or dairy.

MUST-HAVE ITEMS

- Good knives (2 complete sets)
- Cutting boards (2)
- Large stockpot or soup pot
- Small, medium, and large pots or saucepans (2 to 4)
- Skillets (2 to 4, in varying sizes)
- Large Dutch oven or other oven-proof pot with a lid
- Large roasting pan (for meat)
- Cookie sheets (2)
- Rimmed baking sheets, 18-by-13-inch (2)
- Measuring cups (2 sets)
- Mixing bowls (2 sets)
- Muffin tins (2)
- Springform pan
- Wire cooling racks (2)
- Rubber spatulas (1 or 2 each for meat and dairy)
- Metal spatulas (2)
- Mixing spoons (2 or 3 each for meat and dairy)
- Ladles (2)
- Whisks (2)
- Kitchen shears (2)
- Serving utensils (2 sets)
- Food processor (for meat)
- Stand blender (for dairy)
- Immersion blenders (2)
- Microplane zester
- Garlic press

NICE-TO-HAVE ITEMS

- High-powdered blender
- Stand mixer (for baking)
- Citrus juicer
- Cast-iron skillet
- Challah molds

Kashering

Whether you are keeping kosher for the first time or have always kept kosher and are moving into a new home, the kitchen and your cooking utensils need to be kashered. Kashering refers to the process of making an unkosher kitchen kosher, or of making new kitchenware (like pots, silverware, or dishware) kosher.

The steps to kasher a kitchen can be labor-intensive, but they're fairly straightforward. You'll start by removing all nonkosher food from the kitchen. Then, you'll clean the kitchen thoroughly. This includes cleaning the sink, counters, refrigerator, ovens, and stovetop. To clean the counters and sink, you'll need to pour boiling water all over them. The ovens and stove will need to be set on the highest temperature and allowed to burn for a few hours. To kasher pots and utensils, dip them in aluminum pans of boiling water. Once the cleaning is done, the kitchen should not be used for 24 hours.

Kashering an entire kitchen can seem intimidating to those just learning about it. If you're new to the process, a rabbi can come to your home and kasher your kitchen for you. The rabbi will likely show up with a blowtorch, steel wool, cleaning supplies, paper towels, and most likely large aluminum pans. The rabbi will perform the process of kashering the kitchen and help you understand exactly which items can be kashered and which items will need to be replaced.

Once the kitchen is cleaned, designate spaces for meat and dairy. Label cabinets and drawers for meat, dairy, and pareve and put the appropriate kitchenware in each. Some people also label the shelves in their refrigerator. Decide which counters or other surfaces you'll use for milk and which for meat. Last, designate large appliances, like your ovens, dishwasher, and sink (with sink liners, if necessary).

The first time I kashered my kitchen, my husband called the Chabad rabbi to help. While the rabbi was working, I heard a loud noise, looked up, and saw glass flying all across the kitchen. His blowtorch was apparently too tough on my glass cooktop, which shattered in every direction. The story ends happily, though—I got a beautiful stainless-steel cooktop the very next day. Hopefully your kitchen kashering doesn't involve any broken glass, but just know that whatever happens, kashering can be done!

CREATING YOUR KOSHER HOME

Judaism is very much grounded in and around the home, and meals in particular. Entertaining and sharing meals on Shabbat and other holidays bring families, friends, and communities together. Many would agree that one hallmark of a Jewish home is making guests feel welcome and cared for. Part of that hospitality is putting genuine effort and love into preparing food.

Entertaining is naturally woven into any kosher home during Shabbat every week. Shabbat is built around three meals and offers a spiritual time to connect with religion around the dinner table with family and friends. In this way, our spirituality is intertwined with the simple but essential act of nourishing ourselves.

In a kosher, Jewish home, cooking together and eating together help us keep family values and traditions alive. We pass down family recipes and memories and make new ones along the way. The recipes in this book—which range from traditional holiday dishes to family favorites to modern kosher adaptations—reflect the unique bond between Judaism, cooking, and tradition. I love to cook and entertain, and I hope that as you prepare the recipes in this book, that love will shine through.

Sourcing Kosher Foods

These days, it's easier than ever before to get your hands on kosher food. Kosher items are available at almost every grocery store, and most mainstream supermarkets have a designated kosher aisle with basics like grape juice, broth, tea, matzoh, gefilte fish, candy, egg noodles, vinegar, and oil.

Beyond the kosher aisle, you'll have to do a little hunting. More common household items that have a kosher certification, such as flour, sugar, chocolate, snacks, dairy, and other foods, will not always be located in the kosher aisle. For this reason, when shopping at a regular supermarket, check food packaging for kosher certification labels. Some kosher dairy products, for instance, will be marked with a D next to the kosher certification. Other products will be marked with DE, indicating that the product doesn't contain dairy but was processed on equipment that is also used to process dairy.

Many mainstream supermarkets carry a limited selection of kosher meat, poultry, fish, and cheese, but not the full scope. For the most options, your best bet is to go to a kosher supermarket or butcher. In general, if you have access to a kosher market, I highly recommend taking the time to go there—it will make your job much easier and quicker.

The variety of kosher-certified foods grows every day. Many upscale, niche ingredients line the shelves of kosher markets—I recently found some delicious truffle oil and even a gourmet saffron oil. I encourage you to explore your options to the fullest, but rest assured that the recipes in this book rely on basic staple ingredients that won't be difficult to track down.

The Kosher Pantry

Great everyday recipes use a combination of fresh ingredients paired with pantry staples. Here are the items I keep stocked at all times:

- Broths: vegetable and chicken
- Canned beans
- Canned tomatoes (fire-roasted tomatoes and tomatoes with green chilies, such as Ro-Tel, are my go-to essentials)
- Coconut milk
- Condiments: hot sauce, ketchup, mayonnaise, mustard
- Dried herbs and spices: sea salt, ground black pepper, paprika (sweet and smoked), cumin, red pepper flakes, oregano, parsley, cinnamon, garlic powder, onion powder, turmeric, everything bagel seasoning, basil, za'atar, mustard powder, ground ginger
- Grains: rice, brown rice, quinoa, rolled oats, whole-grain pasta, bean pasta
- Honey
- Maple syrup
- Oils: avocado, olive, grapeseed
- Soy sauce
- Vinegars: distilled white, apple cider, rice, balsamic

Storing Kosher Foods

A kosher home requires putting a little bit of extra thought into food preparation and storage. When cooking for Shabbat every week, food must be made in advance and stored properly to last through all three meals. For a holiday or other large gathering, cooking and food prep may span three or more days. Here are my tips for proper storage to prevent spoilage, bacteria, and cross-contamination.

Storing Dairy

Dairy products are best stored on a cold shelf near the back of the refrigerator—consider designating the top shelf of your refrigerator for dairy. If you choose to store dairy in the door of the refrigerator, be mindful that door temperature is a little higher, so products may spoil faster.

Butter can be stored in the refrigerator for up to 3 months, frozen for up to 6 months, or left out on the counter in a butter dish. The current USDA standards indicate that butter can keep at room temperature for up to 2 days. If you want to keep an old-school butter dish out, portion out an amount that you'll finish in 2 days.

Different cheeses need to be stored in different ways. Soft cheese should be consumed within 1 week of opening. Many hard cheeses will keep for over a month—you can safely cut off moldy spots without worrying about contamination. Cheese should always be tightly wrapped. Shredded cheese lasts only a week or so before it may begin to spoil. If frozen, hard or shredded cheeses will keep for 2 to 3 months.

Yogurt and milk that have been opened will usually keep for 4 to 7 days—you'll be able to smell spoilage. Cottage cheese lasts a little longer, 7 to 10 days. Sour cream will last for about 2 weeks. Milk and yogurt can be frozen for up to 1 month, but be warned that their texture will change, so they should be used only in cooking or baking.

Storing Meat

It's safest to store meat in the freezer, properly sealed to keep out air and moisture. When frozen, meat can keep for up to 1 year, but it tastes best when cooked within 4 months. Fresh, uncooked cuts of meat will stay fresh for 3 to 5 days in the refrigerator, while ground meats should be cooked or frozen within 1 to 2 days.

The easiest way to thaw meat is in the refrigerator; otherwise, run it under cold water in the designated meat sink. When thawing or marinating meat, make sure it is well covered to prevent leakage so you can avoid contamination.

Once cooked, meat will last for 3 to 4 days in the refrigerator. This is very helpful in preparing food in advance for Shabbat or longer holidays. For poultry, the above guidelines for freezing and cooking apply. However, note that raw poultry will keep for only 1 to 2 days in the refrigerator.

Storing Fish

Fresh fish will keep in the refrigerator for only 1 to 2 days, and cooked fish will keep for 3 to 4 days. The guidelines for freezing fish vary by type—lean fish (like cod, halibut, and sole) can be frozen for up to 6 months, while fatty fish (like tuna and salmon) are best prepared within 3 months.

Cooked fish (especially smoked fish, like nova or lox) can be frozen for 4 to 6 months and still retain vibrant flavor.

KOSHER CUTS: GET TO KNOW YOUR BUTCHER

Kosher slaughtering of animals uses a specific process called *shechita*. The person who slaughters the animal is called a *shochet*, and they must be a Jewish person who keeps kashrut and has studied kosher and *shechita* laws. The *shochet* uses a sharp knife with no nicks, intended to be humane—done quickly so that the animal does not feel pain.

After being put to death, the animal is checked to see if it can be further labeled as "glatt kosher." *Glatt* means "smooth," so the animal's lungs are checked to ensure they are smooth and free of defects, which could indicate the animal suffered or had an illness. If the lungs are smooth, the animal can be labeled glatt kosher. If they are not, the animal is not kosher.

The meat from the animal is then soaked and salted to remove all blood. The soaked and salted meat is then packaged and sold to the customers. When you shop for kosher meat at the supermarket, look for the "glatt kosher" label. This label is often used in a more general sense to refer to meat that has been produced under strict kashrut guidelines (including draining blood and slaughter).

Although a variety of different cuts of meat are available from kosher butchers, some specific cuts are not kosher, so you won't find them. For example: Cuts from the hind of the animal where the sciatic nerve passes through—no filet mignon!. Most red meat cuts from the front of the animal—like chuck, rib, shoulder, and foreshank—are available (for beef, veal, and lamb). The recipes in this book will usually specify which cut of meat or poultry to use, unless the preparation can be used with many cuts of meat.

Preparing (and Serving!) Kosher Foods

Maintaining a kosher kitchen takes some extra time and forethought, but once you get in the swing of things, it's incredibly rewarding. (Though it's not without its speed bumps—more than once, I've carefully timed when to start cooking a meat meal for Shabbat only to find my kids already in the kitchen making pizza.) So now that I've gone over the nitty-gritty, you should be well-equipped to start cooking. Here are some final tips for success when preparing and serving kosher foods:

▸ Avoid preparing meat and dairy on the same counter or with the same equipment.

▸ Organize your kitchen so that meat and dairy kitchenware are stored (and labeled) in different areas, with a smaller area designated for pareve items like glassware.

▸ Designate separate serving dishes and cutlery for meat and dairy.

▸ Always read the full recipe (or recipes) before you start cooking, to ensure you have all the ingredients on hand and enough time to finish cooking.

▸ Plan your menus so you can cook dairy and meat at separate times.

For Shabbat: According to the Laws of Kashrut, all foods cooked for Shabbat must be finished cooking before sundown on Friday. Here are my tips for timing your food prep for success on Shabbat and other holidays:

Try to buy your groceries for Shabbat on Wednesday or Thursday, to allow yourself plenty of time to cook some dishes ahead of time. I find Thursday evening is a great time to start prepping for Shabbat, especially if you work during the day—it'll make your cooking on Friday a breeze.

Take advantage of adding cold or room-temperature dishes, like salads and sides, to the menu. Many of these can be prepared in their entirety days in advance—or prepare any cooked elements before sundown and assemble the dish when you're ready to eat.

The Shabbat Table

Shabbat dinners will vary depending on the time of year, the occasion, and, most important, the guests at the table. If it's just your family, you might like to make some low-maintenance favorites. If you're having company, you may try something more adventurous, or vice versa—I always test out new recipes on my family before I make them for guests. Whatever you're serving, choose what to make in advance so you're not scrambling at the last minute.

Here, I outline my menu suggestions for a few different Shabbat meals, from the most classic to a holiday menu that pulls out all the stops. All of these menus would be enhanced by including some dips as appetizers: good choices are Garlicky Eggplant Spread (page 118), Red Pepper Spread (page 119), 3-Ingredient Olive Dip (page 121), Shortcut Matbucha (page 122), and Israeli Schug (page 125).

Traditional Shabbat Meal

This old-school Shabbat menu includes my takes on Jewish classics that have been passed down in my family for generations.

→ Classic Chicken Soup (page 52)

→ Red Pepper Spread (page 119)

→ Spiced Carrot Salad (page 48)

→ Grandma Dotty's Brisket (page 82)

→ Jamie's Deli-Style Egg Barley (page 39)

→ Chocolate Chip Mandelbread Squares (page 106)

Modern Shabbat Meal

Beyond the classics, Shabbat is also a great time to enjoy new foods. This updated menu takes cues from modern-day favorites and cuisines from all around the world.

→ Kale Salad with Pear and Pumpkin Seeds (page 42)

→ Lamb Tagine (page 89)

→ Mustard-Spiced Roasted Potatoes (page 40)

→ Shaved Brussels Sprout Slaw (page 47)

→ Tahini Chocolate Chip Blondies (page 113)

Vegetarian Shabbat Meal

Vegetarian meals certainly have a place in kosher households, and many of the dairy and pareve recipes in this book are ideal for putting together a vegetarian Shabbat meal plan.

→ Vegetarian "Crab" Cakes (page 75)

→ Lemony Green Bean Salad (page 46)

→ Curried Lentil Soup (page 56)

→ Peperonata (page 38)

→ Chai Chocolate Mousse (page 107)

Rosh Hashanah or Holiday Meal

Rosh Hashanah, the start of the Jewish new year, marks the beginning of the holiday season in the Jewish calendar. Many Jewish families cook a special meal for the occasion. On Rosh Hashanah, it's custom for Jews to eat sweet foods—like carrots, apples, dates, string beans, pomegranates, and honey—to symbolize a sweet new year. This festive Rosh Hashanah menu certainly fulfills that requirement!

→ Creamy Carrot Soup (page 59)

→ Wilted Spinach Salad with Warm Apples (page 45)

→ Braised Cornish Hens with Dates and Cherries (page 96)

→ Wild Rice and Avocado Salad (page 41)

→ Simple Overnight Marinated Broccoli (page 49)

→ Almost-Any-Fruit Crumble (page 108)

It's also traditional to serve a fish head at the table, symbolizing the "head" of the year (*rosh* means "head" in Hebrew). You always want to be the head and not the tail. In my house, we serve a whole roasted sea bass with the head attached as an appetizer (there's no specific recipe, but if you want to try it, stuff the fish with lemon, garlic, and fresh herbs, rub the outside with olive oil, salt, and black pepper, wrap in foil, and roast at 500°F for 20 minutes).

About the Recipes

The recipes in this book span an array of flavors, ranging from traditional Jewish foods to modern adaptations and dishes from Jewish cuisines around the world. I've also included favorites from my own family, some of which are recipes that were made by my grandmother and passed down to me by my mom. I hope that the recipes in this book will become a part of your own family meals, celebrations, and traditions.

The recipes are divided into sections to streamline choices for weekday, weekend, Shabbat, and holiday meals. Each recipe includes labels to make it easy to find the right dish for any occasion. The labels used in these recipes are:

- ▶ Gluten-Free
- ▶ Great for Shabbat: recipes that have longer prep times but can be easily prepared ahead of time to enjoy on Shabbat
- ▶ Pareve
- ▶ Vegetarian
- ▶ Weeknight: recipes that can be prepared quickly with simple staple ingredients
- ▶ Weekend: recipes that are more involved or have longer cook times, or can be prepared ahead and stored

After each recipe, you'll find various tips, which might be ideas for variations or substitutions for ingredients, cooking techniques, or make-ahead instructions.

I love the recipes in this book, and I'm so excited for you to explore them. So, continue on to the next chapters and check them out—there's something for everyone.

Jamie's Shortcut Shakshuka 22

CHAPTER 2

Breakfast

In a Jewish household, with so much energy focused on cooking Shabbat dinners, breakfast sometimes falls by the wayside. But as a nutritionist, it's always been important to me not to skip what we all know as "the most important meal of the day." For that reason, I've included breakfast recipes that are attainable, not over-the-top, and, above all, delicious. Breakfast can come in many forms, and the recipes in this chapter cover all the bases. There are easy breakfasts to eat on the go, like Trail Mix Breakfast Bars and Lox-and-Onion Egg Muffins, as well as more decadent options for weekend brunches, like Overnight Apple Challah French Toast. Try them all and keep breakfast on the table (so to speak) on busy days and lazy ones alike.

Jamie's Shortcut Shakshuka

PAREVE, VEGETARIAN, WEEKEND

SERVES 6 • PREP TIME: 5 MINUTES / COOK TIME: 20 MINUTES

Shakshuka (eggs stewed in a tomato-and-pepper sauce) is a breakfast favorite, but I don't always have fresh produce on hand to make the traditional version. I just developed this shortcut shakshuka on such a Sunday morning, when I had no fresh bell peppers or tomatoes left after Shabbat. It was a hit: My daughter said it was my best shakshuka ever. For added spice, stir in 1 or 2 teaspoons of Israeli Schug (page 125) when you add the canned tomatoes. Serve with toasted bread to sop up the sauce!

2 tablespoons avocado oil

1 onion, finely diced

1 (10-ounce) can diced tomatoes with green chilies (such as Ro-Tel), undrained

1 (28-ounce) can diced fire-roasted tomatoes, undrained

½ teaspoon sea salt

¼ teaspoon freshly ground black pepper

2 teaspoons ground cumin

6 large eggs

6 slices toasted bread, for serving

1. In a large deep skillet, heat the avocado oil over medium heat. Once the oil is hot, add the onion and sauté for 10 minutes, or until softened and golden brown.

2. Add both cans of tomatoes and their juices to the pan and stir to incorporate. Mix in the salt, pepper, and cumin, reduce the heat to medium-low, and cook the mixture for 5 minutes, or until the sauce comes to a slow boil.

3. Make 6 small wells in the sauce and crack an egg into each well. Cover the pan with the lid and cook for 5 minutes, or until the eggs are just set.

4. Serve the shakshuka immediately, with the toast on the side.

INGREDIENT TIP: For kosher cooking, it's best to crack each egg individually into a measuring cup before transferring it to the sauce to cook. This way, you'll see if the egg has a spot of blood in it before you add it—if it does, it isn't kosher.

Overnight Apple Challah French Toast

GREAT FOR SHABBAT, VEGETARIAN, WEEKEND

SERVES 4 TO 6 • PREP TIME: 30 MINUTES, PLUS OVERNIGHT
TO SOAK / COOK TIME: 40 MINUTES

Everyone loves challah—and what's more decadent and delicious than overnight challah French toast? This almost bread pudding–like recipe brings new life to leftover store-bought or homemade challah. This is a great break-the-fast dish for Yom Kippur—it's warm, sweet, and super-satisfying. My family likes to use apples in this recipe, but bananas would work equally well. Leftover Cinnamon Crumb Challah (page 23) works wonderfully in this recipe.

1 cup packed light brown sugar

8 tablespoons (1 stick) unsalted butter

2 tablespoons honey

4 apples, peeled, cored, and thinly sliced

8 large eggs

2 cups milk

1 teaspoon vanilla extract

1 teaspoon ground cinnamon

9 slices day-old challah, cubed
  (5 to 6 cups)

1. In a small saucepan, combine the brown sugar, butter, and honey. Cook over low heat for 2 minutes, or until the sugar dissolves and the mixture is smooth.

2. Pour the sugar mixture into an ungreased 9-by-13-inch baking dish. Arrange the sliced apples on top and set the dish aside.

3. In a large bowl, with a whisk or a hand mixer, beat the eggs, milk, vanilla, and cinnamon until thoroughly incorporated.

4. Spread the cubed challah in an even layer over the apples in the baking dish. Pour the egg mixture over the challah. Use a spatula to press down on the challah to ensure it is thoroughly soaked. Cover the dish with aluminum foil and refrigerate overnight.

5. The next morning, remove the dish from the refrigerator and preheat the oven to 350°F.

6. Bake for 45 minutes, or until it is puffed up and golden brown on top.

7. Cut the challah French toast into squares and use a spatula to serve. Enjoy immediately. Store leftovers in an airtight container in the refrigerator for up to 2 days.

INGREDIENT TIP: To make this dish pareve, you can use a plant-based milk instead of dairy milk and use coconut oil instead of butter.

Trail Mix Breakfast Bars

GREAT FOR SHABBAT, PAREVE, VEGETARIAN

MAKES 12 BARS • PREP TIME: 10 MINUTES, PLUS 30 MINUTES
TO COOL / COOK TIME: 15 MINUTES

Trail mix is already a good-to-go snack, but these no-bake cereal trail mix bars take it to the next level—they're kind of like a healthier Rice Krispies Treat. I like to prepare these crispy, chewy bars in large batches and keep my freezer well stocked with them at all times. They're filling enough to eat as a quick breakfast—my teenagers often grab them on the way to school.

3 cups Rice Krispies cereal

3 cups Cheerios cereal

1½ cups dried cherries

¾ cup sunflower seeds

1 cup pareve chocolate chips

1 cup honey

½ cup sugar

2 cups almond butter

1 teaspoon vanilla extract

1. Line a 9-by-13-inch baking pan with parchment paper to come up all sides (this will make it easy to remove the bars from the pan after baking).

2. In a large bowl, combine the Rice Krispies, Cheerios, dried cherries, sunflower seeds, and chocolate chips. Mix to incorporate and set aside.

3. In a medium saucepan, combine the honey and sugar. Heat the mixture over medium-high heat for 5 to 10 minutes, stirring often, until it reaches a boil (watch it closely so it doesn't burn). Once boiling, add the almond butter and vanilla and cook, stirring continuously, for 2 minutes, until the almond butter is melted. Remove the saucepan from the heat.

4. Pour the almond butter mixture over the cereal mixture and toss until thoroughly coated. Transfer the entire mixture to the baking pan and press it into an even layer. Let cool for at least 30 minutes.

5. Once completely cooled, cut into 12 bars and serve. Store leftovers in an airtight container at room temperature for up to 1 week. (Alternatively, wrap individual bars tightly in plastic wrap or aluminum foil and freeze for up to 1 month.)

VARIATION TIP: This recipe is versatile—it works well with most cereals, any nut butter, and any dried fruit (or nuts instead of chocolate chips). Try experimenting with different combinations to find your favorites!

Lox-and-Onion Egg Muffins

GLUTEN-FREE, WEEKEND, WEEKNIGHT

MAKES 12 MUFFINS (SERVES 6) • PREP TIME: 15 MINUTES / COOK TIME: 20 MINUTES

These egg muffins are my convenience-minded spin on lox, eggs, and onions, a classic Jewish comfort food and one of my husband's favorites. I like to keep batches of these egg "muffins" in the freezer for my teenagers to microwave for an easy after-school snack. These will keep for up to 1 month in the freezer—to reheat, simply microwave for 1 to 2 minutes.

Cooking spray

2 teaspoons unsalted butter

1 onion, finely diced

1 (10-ounce) package lox or nova, finely chopped

8 large eggs

1 tablespoon milk

¼ teaspoon sea salt

½ teaspoon freshly ground black pepper

2 tablespoons cream cheese

1. Preheat the oven to 350°F. Mist a standard muffin tin with cooking spray.

2. In a medium skillet, melt the butter over medium heat. Add the onion and sauté, stirring occasionally, for 5 minutes, until soft and translucent.

3. Reduce the heat to low, add the lox to the pan, and cook over low heat for 1 to 2 minutes, until just heated through. Remove from the heat and set aside to cool.

4. In a medium bowl, whisk together the eggs, milk, salt, and pepper until well combined.

5. Divide the egg mixture evenly among the muffin cups. Evenly portion the lox-onion mixture into the muffin cups.

6. Bake the egg muffins for 15 to 20 minutes, until the eggs are set. While the muffins are still warm, top each one with ½ teaspoon of the cream cheese.

7. Serve the egg muffins hot. If freezing, let cool to room temperature, then wrap the muffins individually in plastic wrap and freeze for up to 1 month.

INGREDIENT TIP: To make this recipe pareve, substitute avocado oil or olive oil for the butter and use vegan cream cheese.

Strawberry-Almond Overnight Oats

GLUTEN-FREE, GREAT FOR SHABBAT, PAREVE, VEGETARIAN

SERVES 4 • PREP TIME: 10 MINUTES, PLUS OVERNIGHT TO SOAK

Breakfast doesn't get any easier than this. These low-effort, high-reward overnight oats are simple but versatile—the possibilities for toppings are endless. Strawberries and almonds are my favorite mix-ins, but other fresh fruits, chopped nuts, chocolate chips, and shredded coconut all make lovely alternatives. This is a great recipe for a busy workday or a Shabbat morning—just make one mason jar for each person in your family.

1 cup gluten-free rolled oats

1½ cups unsweetened plant-based milk of your choice (such as soy, oat, or almond)

2 tablespoons honey or maple syrup

½ teaspoon vanilla extract

1 cup chopped strawberries

¼ cup sliced almonds

1. Divide the oats, milk, honey, and vanilla evenly among four 1-pint mason jars. Stir vigorously to combine.

2. Divide the strawberries and almonds evenly among the jars and stir to incorporate. (Alternatively, skip this step for now, and add the toppings just before serving.)

3. Cover the mason jars with airtight lids and refrigerate overnight. (If making for future breakfasts, you can keep the oats refrigerated for up to 2 days.)

4. The next morning, if the toppings were held back, add them now. Enjoy cold, or microwave for 1 to 2 minutes and enjoy hot.

VARIATION TIP: For a dairy meal, swap out the plant-based milk for 1 cup whole milk and ½ cup Greek yogurt—it's an even richer and more decadent breakfast.

Egg-in-a-Pita with Tahini

PAREVE, VEGETARIAN, WEEKEND

SERVES 2 • PREP TIME: 5 MINUTES / COOK TIME: 10 MINUTES

Growing up, my favorite breakfast was one I ate at my friend Aviva's house. The morning after our sleepovers, her mom would make us egg-in-a-hole: a fried slice of bread with a sunny-side-up egg cooked in the middle. This is my ode to that childhood favorite, made on crispy fried pita and topped with tahini and everything bagel seasoning (a mix of poppy seeds, sesame seeds, dried garlic, dried onion, and salt).

2 pita breads

2 tablespoons avocado oil

2 large eggs

1 teaspoon everything bagel seasoning

¼ cup tahini

1. Use a round cookie cutter or the rim of a glass to make a 2- to 3-inch hole in the center of each pita.

2. In a large skillet, heat the avocado oil over medium heat until hot. Add the pitas to the pan and cook for 1 minute on each side, or until just golden brown. Add a cracked egg to the hole in the center of each pita. Sprinkle generously with the everything bagel seasoning.

3. Cover the pan and cook for 3 to 5 minutes, depending on how you like your eggs cooked.

4. Remove from the heat, drizzle generously with the tahini, and serve immediately.

VARIATION TIP: For added heat, use hot sauce instead of (or in addition to) the tahini.

Blueberry Baked Oatmeal Squares

GLUTEN-FREE, GREAT FOR SHABBAT,
PAREVE, VEGETARIAN

MAKES 12 SQUARES (SERVES 6 TO 12) • PREP TIME: 15 MINUTES /
COOK TIME: 45 MINUTES

This recipe came out of my love for oatmeal raisin cookies. Its high fiber and protein content make it nutritious, but it's really almost dessert-like—a healthy breakfast treat. These squares are a great make-ahead breakfast for Shabbat morning, though it's hard to eat just one! I like to make a double batch and freeze the extras individually to enjoy on the go. (To reheat, microwave for 1 to 2 minutes.)

Cooking spray

2 cups gluten-free rolled oats

2 cups boiling water

1 (13-ounce) can full-fat coconut milk

1 large egg, beaten

½ cup maple syrup

2 cups blueberries

2 teaspoons ground cinnamon

1 teaspoon vanilla extract

1. Preheat the oven to 350°F. Mist a 9-by-13-inch baking dish with cooking spray.

2. In a large heatproof bowl, combine the oats, boiling water, and coconut milk and stir to combine. Add the egg and stir vigorously, working quickly to prevent it from cooking whole. Add the maple syrup, blueberries, cinnamon, and vanilla and stir thoroughly to incorporate.

3. Transfer the mixture to the prepared baking dish and spread it into an even layer. Bake for 45 minutes, or until golden brown on top.

4. Cut into 12 squares before serving. To freeze, cool the squares for 30 minutes before wrapping them individually in foil or plastic wrap, then freeze for up to 2 months.

VARIATION TIP: To boost the protein content of these bars, add 1 scoop of pareve protein powder or ¼ cup hemp hearts when you add the blueberries.

Banana Pancakes

VEGETARIAN, WEEKEND

MAKES 12 PANCAKES (SERVES 3 OR 4) • PREP TIME: 10 MINUTES /
COOK TIME: 15 MINUTES

Banana pancakes are a crowd-pleaser on lazy Sunday mornings. These luxurious-feeling pancakes come together easily, so you can sleep in and still have them ready in no time. This recipe is great for using up bananas that are a little too soft to eat—the overripe bananas will add even more sweetness. For a treat, mix ½ cup pareve chocolate chips into the batter. Be prepared—everyone will want seconds!

1 cup all-purpose flour

¼ teaspoon sea salt

1 teaspoon ground cinnamon

1 teaspoon baking powder

3 bananas

4 large eggs

2 tablespoons unsalted butter

Maple syrup, for serving

1. In a large bowl, combine the flour, salt, cinnamon, and baking powder and stir to incorporate.

2. In a medium bowl, mash the bananas with a fork until smooth. Add the eggs and mix until fully incorporated. Add the banana mixture to the dry mixture and stir until just combined.

3. In a medium skillet, melt 1 tablespoon of the butter over low heat. Once the butter is melted, increase the heat to medium and spoon ⅛ cup (2 tablespoons) of the batter into the pan. (You can cook multiple pancakes at a time—just don't overcrowd the pan.) Cook the pancakes on the first side until bubbles form across the tops, about 2 minutes. Flip the pancakes and cook until golden brown on both sides, about 1 more minute. Transfer the pancakes to a plate.

4. Repeat with the remaining batter, using the remaining 1 tablespoon butter to regrease the pan after you've cooked half the batter.

5. Serve the pancakes warm, drizzled with maple syrup. Refrigerate leftover pancakes in a resealable plastic bag for 1 to 3 days. To reheat, microwave individual pancakes for 1 minute.

VARIATION TIP: To make gluten-free banana pancakes, substitute the same amount of buckwheat flour. For pareve pancakes, replace the butter with 2 tablespoons coconut oil. For a vegan version, you can actually omit the eggs—just know the pancakes will be a bit softer, so flip them carefully.

Overnight Vegetarian Breakfast Casserole

GREAT FOR SHABBAT, VEGETARIAN, WEEKEND

SERVES 4 TO 6 • PREP TIME: 20 MINUTES, PLUS OVERNIGHT
TO SOAK / COOK TIME: 1 HOUR

My mother made this dish every year for our Yom Kippur "break-the-fast" meal. It was perfect for the occasion: She'd prepare it the day before our fast, and 45 minutes before the fast ended, she'd put it in the oven so it would be ready for us right away. Today, I take it out of the refrigerator 2 hours before the fast ends so it can come to room temperature. Once the fast is over, I pop it in the oven. The ingredients might seem like a lot, but rest assured that everything soaks into the bread, and it tastes sensational.

Cooking spray

2 loaves day-old bread, cubed (8 or 9 cups)

10 large eggs, beaten

4 cups milk

1½ teaspoons mustard powder

½ teaspoons sea salt

¼ teaspoon freshly ground black pepper

1 (8-ounce) package cremini mushrooms, sliced

2 cups cherry tomatoes, halved

6 scallions, finely chopped

2 cups shredded cheese or nondairy cheese of your choice (I recommend cheddar)

1. Mist a 9-by-13-inch glass baking dish (or a large single-use aluminum roasting pan) with cooking spray. Spread the cubed bread over the bottom of the pan in an even layer.

2. In a large bowl, whisk together the eggs, milk, mustard powder, salt, and pepper.

3. Pour the egg mixture over the bread in the baking dish. Use a spatula to press down on the bread to ensure it is thoroughly soaked. Evenly distribute the mushrooms, cherry tomatoes, and scallions over the bread. Sprinkle with the cheese. Cover the dish with aluminum foil and refrigerate overnight.

4. The next morning, preheat the oven to 325°F.

5. Bake the casserole for 45 minutes, then remove the foil and bake for an additional 15 minutes, or until the cheese is bubbling and golden brown on the edges.

6. Serve the casserole hot. Store leftovers tightly wrapped in the dish (or in an airtight container) in the refrigerator for up to 2 days. Reheat in the oven at 300°F for 20 to 30 minutes, until heated through, or microwave single portions for 1 to 2 minutes.

Chocolate Chip Muffins

GLUTEN-FREE, GREAT FOR SHABBAT, PAREVE,
VEGETARIAN, WEEKEND

MAKES 12 MUFFINS (SERVES 6 TO 12) • PREP TIME: 15 MINUTES,
PLUS 10 MINUTES TO COOL / COOK TIME: 15 TO 18 MINUTES

These decadent-but-actually-nutritious muffins are a great make-ahead breakfast for Shabbat mornings and are a crowd-pleaser if you have guests. They're packed with nutrients and gluten-free by design. Feel free to adapt this recipe to fit what you have on hand—swap the applesauce for 2 mashed bananas, substitute chopped nuts for the chocolate, or use butter instead of coconut oil (if dairy ingredients are permitted).

⅓ cup gluten-free rolled oats

1 cup applesauce

3 large eggs

3 tablespoons coconut oil, melted

1 teaspoon vanilla extract

⅓ cup nut butter of your choice

1 teaspoon ground cinnamon

½ teaspoon ground nutmeg

½ teaspoon baking soda

½ teaspoon baking powder

¼ teaspoon sea salt

1 cup pareve chocolate chips

1. Preheat the oven to 350°F. Line a standard muffin tin with paper liners.

2. In a blender or food processor, grind the oats until they reach a fine, flour-like consistency. Set aside.

3. In a large bowl, mix together the applesauce, eggs, coconut oil, vanilla, and nut butter until well combined.

4. Add the ground-up oats, cinnamon, nutmeg, baking soda, baking powder, and salt and mix until incorporated. Gently fold in the chocolate chips, without overmixing.

5. Divide the batter evenly among the prepared muffin cups. Bake for 15 to 18 minutes, until a toothpick inserted into the center of a muffin comes out clean.

6. Let the muffins cool in the tin (or on a wire rack) for 10 minutes before serving.

7. Serve hot. Store leftover muffins in an airtight container at room temperature for 1 to 2 days. To freeze, cool the muffins completely, wrap tightly in plastic wrap or foil, and freeze for up to 2 months.

VARIATION TIP: You can use this same batter to make a delicious microwave mug cake that cooks in no time. To do so, mist the inside of a microwave-safe coffee mug with cooking spray, fill it halfway with batter, and microwave for 1 to 2 minutes, until a toothpick inserted into the center comes out clean.

Kale Salad with Pear and Pumpkin Seeds 42

CHAPTER 3

Sides and Salads

The recipes in this chapter cover a broad spectrum, from cool, refreshing summer salads (Lemony Green Bean Salad and Spiced Carrot Salad) to hearty oven-roasted sides (Mustard-Spiced Roasted Potatoes and Jamie's Deli-Style Egg Barley) and everything in between. (I know "in between" sounds like a crazy claim, but if you don't believe me, try the Wilted Spinach Salad with Warm Apples.) A few of the sides are on the more elaborate end, like the Eggplant Latkes with Za'atar Garlic Hummus, but most are simple to prepare and designed to be quick, with the intent to make Shabbat meal prep as manageable as possible. I love them all, and I hope you'll find them palate-pleasing accompaniments to any meal.

Eggplant Latkes with Za'atar Garlic Hummus

PAREVE, VEGETARIAN, WEEKEND

SERVES 4 TO 6 • PREP TIME: 30 MINUTES / COOK TIME: 45 MINUTES

This healthier spin on potato latkes tastes just as delicious, I promise! Eggplant takes on the perfect texture for these light and crispy yet filling fritters. Don't skip the initial step of salting the eggplant and letting it rest—it allows some of the moisture to drain, preventing the latkes from getting soggy. Making the za'atar hummus is worth the extra couple of steps and elevates this dish to the next level. A thrifty tip: Save the liquid from the can of chickpeas to make Chai Chocolate Mousse (page 107).

For the latke mixture

2 medium eggplants, peeled and diced

1 teaspoon sea salt

3 large eggs

1½ cups unsweetened almond milk

1 cup cornmeal

Scant ½ cup fine dried bread crumbs

2 tablespoons olive oil

For the za'atar garlic hummus

1 (15-ounce) can chickpeas, drained and rinsed

2 garlic cloves, peeled

½ cup water

Juice of ½ lemon

2 tablespoons olive oil

⅔ cup tahini

1 tablespoon ground cumin

3 tablespoons za'atar

1 teaspoon sea salt

For finishing

¾ cup avocado oil (or as needed)

1. **To make the latke mixture:** Place the eggplant in a large colander and sprinkle it with the salt. Set the colander over a plate and let stand for 15 minutes to drain.

2. Meanwhile, in a large bowl, combine the eggs, almond milk, cornmeal, and bread crumbs.

3. Rinse the eggplant to wash away the salt and press down on it with a paper towel to pat away excess water. (You'll know the eggplant is ready once no more water is released.)

4. In a large skillet, heat the olive oil over medium heat. Add the eggplant and cook, stirring often, for about 15 minutes, until the eggplant is browned and softened.

5. Remove the eggplant from the heat and mash it using a wooden spoon or in a food processor. Set aside to cool for 5 to 10 minutes. (Hold on to the skillet.)

6. **To make the za'atar garlic hummus:** In a food processor, combine the chickpeas, garlic, water, lemon juice, olive oil, tahini, cumin, za'atar, and salt. Pulse until smooth. Serve at room temperature or chilled.

7. **To finish the latkes:** Stir the cooled eggplant into the egg mixture and mix until fully incorporated. Form the mixture into 2-inch balls and flatten them slightly into patties. Place the patties on a baking sheet or wire rack.

8. Line a baking sheet or wire rack with paper towels and set it near the stove.

9. Pour ¼ inch of avocado oil into the skillet you used for the eggplant and heat the oil over medium-high heat. Once hot, fry the latkes for 3 minutes on each side, or until golden brown. Set the latkes on the paper towels to drain. If serving later, arrange the latkes on a parchment-lined baking sheet and keep warm in a 200°F oven for up to 3 hours.

10. Serve the latkes hot, with the za'atar hummus for dipping. Store leftover latkes in an airtight container in the refrigerator for 2 to 3 days; leftover hummus will keep in an airtight container in the refrigerator for up to 1 week.

VARIATION TIP: If you don't have eggplant on hand, you can make latkes with the same amount of shredded zucchini or even riced cauliflower. If using zucchini, you can skip steps 1 and 3. If using riced cauliflower, you can skip steps 1 and 3 and there's no need to mash it after cooking.

Peperonata

SERVES 4 • PREP TIME: 10 MINUTES / COOK TIME: 20 MINUTES

Peperonata is a simple but sophisticated Italian dish usually prepared during the summer, when peppers and tomatoes are at peak season. This version is my attempt to replicate a peperonata I tasted many summers ago, and I think I've got it down. This is a true set-it-and-forget-it dish that's great for Friday Shabbat dinners—once you get through the initial prep work, it will practically cook itself.

2 tablespoons olive oil

2 red onions, thinly sliced

6 sweet bell peppers (such as red, yellow, or orange), thinly sliced

4 garlic cloves, minced

4 plum tomatoes, sliced into thin rounds

1 tablespoon dried oregano

1 teaspoon sea salt

½ teaspoon freshly ground black pepper

1 teaspoon distilled white vinegar

1. Spread the olive oil over the bottom of a large, deep skillet. Layer the vegetables in the pan in the following order: onions, bell peppers, garlic, tomatoes. Sprinkle the top with the oregano, salt, and black pepper.

2. Place the pan over medium heat and let the vegetables cook down for about 20 minutes. If you notice burning, turn the heat to medium-low and stir gently to remove any stuck bits, if necessary.

3. Once the vegetables are soft, remove the pan from the heat, add the vinegar, and toss to incorporate. Serve the peperonata hot, at room temperature, or chilled. Store leftovers in an airtight container in the refrigerator for up to 3 days.

VARIATION TIP: Peperonata is a super-versatile leftover. Serve it cold or at room temperature atop greens, sprinkled with pine nuts and drizzled with Perfect Vinaigrette (page 120). Or, serve it hot, alongside pasta topped with Homemade Savory Marinara Sauce (page 124).

Jamie's Deli-Style Egg Barley

GREAT FOR SHABBAT, PAREVE, VEGETARIAN, WEEKEND

SERVES 4 TO 6 • PREP TIME: 10 MINUTES / COOK TIME: 1 HOUR

Egg barley is a staple of old-school Jewish delis everywhere. It's my husband's favorite Shabbat side, so over the years I've perfected my own at-home version. The name can be deceiving, since there's no egg and no barley—instead, this recipe uses toasted barley-shaped egg pasta, available in the kosher section of most supermarkets. This dish stores well in the refrigerator for a few days, so it's perfect to make ahead to enjoy all Shabbat long.

1 (12-ounce) package toasted barley-shaped egg pasta (I recommend Manischewitz brand)

1 (8-ounce) package mushrooms, diced

1 (2-ounce) packet onion soup mix

½ cup grapeseed oil

1 (32-ounce) box vegetable broth

1. Preheat the oven to 350°F.

2. In a 9-by-13-inch glass baking dish, combine the pasta, mushrooms, onion soup mix, grapeseed oil, and broth. Stir to combine.

3. Bake, uncovered, for 1 hour, or until all the liquid has been absorbed. Serve warm or at room temperature. Store leftovers in an airtight container in the refrigerator for up to 5 days.

INGREDIENT TIP: If you don't have vegetable broth on hand, you can substitute chicken broth or even water in a pinch.

Mustard-Spiced Roasted Potatoes

GLUTEN-FREE, GREAT FOR SHABBAT,
PAREVE, VEGETARIAN

SERVES 4 TO 6 • PREP TIME: 15 MINUTES / COOK TIME: 45 MINUTES

We go through a lot of potatoes in my house, and I'm always trying to find new ways to prepare them. This oven-roasted recipe was inspired by my family's love of salt-and-vinegar potato chips. You could also serve these as fries—just cut the potatoes into thin strips instead of cubes. You can make this dish up to 2 days ahead, since it keeps well in the refrigerator and reheats beautifully.

½ cup Dijon mustard

3 tablespoons olive oil

2 tablespoons distilled white vinegar

4 garlic cloves, minced

1 tablespoon dried oregano

1 teaspoon sea salt

½ teaspoon freshly ground black pepper

3 pounds small red potatoes, cubed

1. Preheat the oven to 425°F. Line an 18-by-13-inch baking sheet with parchment paper.

2. In a large bowl, combine the mustard, olive oil, vinegar, garlic, oregano, salt, and pepper. Add the potatoes to the bowl and toss to thoroughly coat.

3. Arrange the seasoned potatoes on the prepared pan and roast for 45 minutes, or until the potatoes are golden brown.

4. Serve hot. Store leftovers in an airtight container in the refrigerator for up to 5 days. To reheat, bake at 300°F for 20 minutes, or until crispy.

INGREDIENT TIP: I use small red potatoes because they have thin skin that doesn't need to be peeled, but you can use any potatoes you'd like. Note that thick-skinned varieties like russet potatoes may need to roast for 5 to 10 minutes longer.

Wild Rice and Avocado Salad

GLUTEN-FREE, GREAT FOR SHABBAT,
PAREVE, VEGETARIAN

SERVES 4 TO 6 • PREP TIME: 15 MINUTES / COOK TIME: 55 MINUTES

This versatile wild rice salad is the perfect complement to any meal and is easy to dress up (try adding seasonal fresh or dried fruit). Don't skip rinsing the rice—it removes excess starch, which helps the final dish come out light rather than gluey.

2 cups wild rice

2 tablespoons avocado oil

1 small onion, finely diced

4 cups boiling water

4 scallions, sliced, for serving

¼ cup Perfect Vinaigrette (page 120)

2 avocados, diced

1. Put the wild rice in a bowl and run it under cold water, using your hands to swish it around, until the water runs clear. Drain the rice and set aside.

2. In a large soup pot, heat the avocado oil over medium heat. Once the oil is hot, add the onion and sauté for 5 minutes, or until soft.

3. Add the rice to the pot and toss with the onions to combine. Add the boiling water and stir to incorporate. Cook over medium heat, allowing it to come to a boil, for about 5 minutes, until almost all the water has been absorbed. Cover the pot, reduce the heat to low, and simmer for 10 minutes.

4. Remove from the heat and let the rice stand, covered, for 30 minutes—this will allow it to soften.

5. Toss the wild rice with the scallions and vinaigrette. Top the dressed salad with the avocados and serve. The dressed salad will keep in an airtight container in the refrigerator for up to 2 days.

MAKE-AHEAD TIP: To make this dish to serve later, cook the wild rice as directed. Store the rice separate from the vinaigrette and don't cut the scallions and avocados until ready to serve. Dress the rice and garnish as directed.

Kale Salad with Pear and Pumpkin Seeds

GLUTEN-FREE, PAREVE, VEGETARIAN, WEEKNIGHT

SERVES 4 • PREP TIME: 20 MINUTES

This is a great recipe to make if you have little helpers in the kitchen. You can have your kids massage the kale with their (washed) hands, which is fun for them and makes a great salad for all to enjoy. To massage the kale, rub it between your fingers for a few minutes with olive oil, lemon juice, and salt, which helps break it down. Don't skip this step—it makes all the difference between a rough, dry, bland kale salad and a delicious, tender-but-still-crunchy one.

1 bunch curly kale, washed, stems and midribs removed

4 tablespoons olive oil, divided

1 lemon, halved

¼ teaspoon sea salt

1½ tablespoons maple syrup

½ teaspoon freshly ground black pepper

½ cup pumpkin seeds

2 pears, cored and thinly sliced

1. Slice or tear the kale leaves into bite-size pieces and place in a large bowl.

2. Drizzle 1½ tablespoons of the oil into the bowl all over the kale. Squeeze the juice from one lemon half into the bowl and sprinkle with the salt. Using your fingertips, massage the kale for 3 minutes, or until it softens—it should turn a brighter green color.

3. In a small bowl, combine the remaining 2½ tablespoons olive oil, the juice from the remaining lemon half, the maple syrup, and the pepper. Set the dressing aside.

4. When ready to serve, toss the dressing with the kale to thoroughly coat it. Top individual servings with the pumpkin seeds and sliced pears.

VARIATION TIP: If pears aren't in season, you can top this salad with almost any seasonal fruit—I recommend halved grapes, sliced fresh figs, or diced peaches, nectarines, or mango.

Sweet Potato Bean Salad

GLUTEN-FREE, GREAT FOR SHABBAT, PAREVE, VEGETARIAN

SERVES 4 • PREP TIME: 30 MINUTES, PLUS 30 MINUTES TO COOL /
COOK TIME: 20 MINUTES

This sweet potato salad is healthy, hearty, and delicious—what could be better? Sweet potatoes are loaded with vitamins A, B, and C and contain potassium, manganese, and fiber. I like to make this salad to serve as a side at Shabbat lunch. If making this for Shabbat, cook the potatoes, chop the vegetables, and make the vinaigrette a day ahead. Then you can toss all the ingredients together quickly on Shabbat morning.

4 sweet potatoes, peeled and cubed

1 red onion, finely chopped

2 teaspoons chopped fresh parsley

1 (15-ounce) can red kidney beans, drained and rinsed

¼ cup Perfect Vinaigrette (page 120)

1. Put the sweet potatoes in a medium pot and add water to cover them entirely. Bring to a boil over high heat. Boil for 20 minutes, or until the potatoes are tender but not falling apart. Drain and set aside to cool for at least 30 minutes.

2. Meanwhile, in a large bowl, combine the onion, parsley, and beans.

3. Once the sweet potatoes are fully cooled, add them to the bowl with the onion and beans and toss to incorporate.

4. When ready to serve, dress with the vinaigrette and toss to coat. Serve at room temperature or chilled. Store leftovers in an airtight container in the refrigerator for up to 3 days.

Wilted Spinach Salad with Warm Apples

GLUTEN-FREE, PAREVE, VEGETARIAN

SERVES 4 • PREP TIME: 15 MINUTES / COOK TIME: 15 MINUTES

I love to make this salad during the fall, when I can choose from a variety of local apples all at peak season. The timing works out, since it's also an excellent dish for Rosh Hashanah. Warm apples and onions on a salad might seem unusual, but trust the process—they cause the spinach to wilt slightly, making for a melt-in-your-mouth texture and surprisingly hearty flavor. If you don't have sunflower seeds, pumpkin seeds or chopped walnuts are great substitutes.

5 cups baby spinach, rinsed

Juice of 1 lemon

1 garlic clove, minced

¼ teaspoon sea salt

¼ teaspoon freshly ground black pepper

5 tablespoons olive oil, divided

1 small onion, chopped

4 apples, sliced

½ cup sunflower seeds

1. Place the spinach in a large bowl and set aside.

2. In a small bowl, combine the lemon juice, garlic, salt, and pepper. Whisk in 3 tablespoons of the olive oil until fully incorporated.

3. Pour half of the dressing over the spinach and toss to combine, reserving the remaining dressing for serving.

4. In a large skillet, heat the remaining 2 tablespoons olive oil over medium heat. Once the oil is hot, add the onion and cook, stirring occasionally, for 8 to 10 minutes, until slightly caramelized.

5. Add the apples to the pan and sauté, stirring occasionally, for 5 minutes, until softened.

6. Add the sunflower seeds to the pan and toss just to combine, then remove from the heat to prevent the seeds from burning.

7. Add the warm apple mixture to the bowl with the spinach and toss to combine—the spinach should wilt slightly. Toss the salad with the remaining dressing and serve immediately.

VARIATION TIP: This salad also pairs well with goat cheese sprinkled on top—try serving it as a festive side for a dairy meal, such as a Yom Tov lunch.

Lemony Green Bean Salad

GLUTEN-FREE, GREAT FOR SHABBAT,
PAREVE, VEGETARIAN

SERVES 4 • PREP TIME: 20 MINUTES / COOK TIME: 5 MINUTES

For this salad, fresh green beans make all the difference. I like to parboil the beans so they retain their crunch and take on a bright green hue. Celery and cucumber provide added bite, making this salad a refreshing side to serve on a hot day. If you like the flavor of anise (it tastes almost like licorice), you can add a sliced fennel bulb—it's super crunchy like the other vegetables and adds wonderful depth of flavor.

1 pound green beans, ends trimmed

¼ cup olive oil

2 tablespoons fresh lemon juice

¼ teaspoon sea salt

¼ teaspoon freshly ground black pepper

4 celery stalks, sliced

1 cucumber, halved and sliced

1 small red onion, halved and sliced

2 tablespoons chopped fresh flat-leaf parsley

1. Boil a kettle of water. Place the green beans in a large pot. Once the water is boiling, pour it over the beans to just cover them. Let the beans parboil for 5 minutes—they should turn bright green, but still be crunchy. Keep an eye on them to prevent them from overcooking and becoming soggy. Drain them and run under cool water to cool them and stop the cooking.

2. Meanwhile, in a small bowl, whisk together the olive oil, lemon juice, salt, and pepper. Set the dressing aside.

3. In a large bowl, combine the celery, cucumber, onion, and parsley. Add the cooled beans to the bowl and toss to combine.

4. When ready to serve, toss the vegetables with the dressing. Serve immediately.

INGREDIENT TIP: To save time, purchase pretrimmed string beans or haricots verts, available at most supermarkets.

Shaved Brussels Sprout Slaw

GLUTEN-FREE, GREAT FOR SHABBAT,
PAREVE, VEGETARIAN

SERVES 4 TO 6 • PREP TIME: 10 MINUTES, PLUS 30 MINUTES TO REST

I wanted to call this a "grown-up" slaw, but the truth is, my kids love it, too. Brussels sprouts are heartier than cabbage, giving this slaw a crunchier texture than a traditional cabbage slaw. Brussels sprouts are high in fiber, vitamins, and minerals, making this salad a winner for flavor as well as health benefits. Preparing this dish ahead of time is key—it allows the Brussels sprouts and cabbage to soak up the honey-mustard dressing, making them flavorful and tender.

¼ cup olive oil

2 tablespoons honey

2 teaspoons Dijon mustard

½ teaspoon sea salt

¼ teaspoon freshly ground black pepper

8 ounces Brussels sprouts

1 (8-ounce) package shredded cabbage

4 scallions, finely chopped

½ cup slivered almonds

1. In a small bowl, whisk together the olive oil, honey, mustard, salt, and pepper. Set the dressing aside.

2. Cut the stem ends off the Brussels sprouts, then halve them through the core. Slice each half into very thin strips. (Alternatively, use a food processor with the slicing blade.)

3. In a large bowl, combine the Brussels sprouts and cabbage and toss to combine. Add the scallions and almonds and toss to combine. Add the dressing and toss to coat.

4. Refrigerate the slaw for 30 minutes before serving to allow the flavors to develop and the greens to soften. Serve chilled.

INGREDIENT TIP: Kosher markets usually don't carry preshredded Brussels sprouts, they're time-intensive to check for kosher certification. They are sold preshredded in other grocery stores (like Trader Joe's), but know that they won't be kosher-certified.

Spiced Carrot Salad

GLUTEN-FREE, GREAT FOR SHABBAT, PAREVE,
VEGETARIAN

SERVES 4 • PREP TIME: 20 MINUTES / COOK TIME: 20 MINUTES

This carrot salad is Moroccan in origin, but it's now popular in Israeli cuisine and in Sephardic Jewish communities around the world. It is often served as one of many *mezzes*, small dishes served in an assortment as an appetizer course, common in eastern Mediterranean cuisines. This recipe uses Israeli Schug, an Israeli condiment (originally from Yemen) that is sold at almost all kosher markets.

2 pounds carrots

4 garlic cloves, minced

2 teaspoons paprika

1½ tablespoons ground cumin

1 teaspoon Israeli Schug (page 125) or any store-bought schug

½ cup fresh lemon juice (from 3 to 4 lemons)

3 tablespoons olive oil

2 tablespoons chopped fresh parsley

1. Bring a large pot of water to a boil over medium-high heat. Add the carrots and cook for 20 minutes, or until just fork-tender but not falling apart.

2. Drain the carrots and run them under cold water to cool them down and stop the cooking. Once cool enough to handle, slice the carrots into ¼-inch rounds.

3. Transfer the carrots to a medium bowl. Add the garlic, paprika, cumin, schug, and lemon juice. Toss to combine.

4. When ready to serve, dress the salad with the olive oil and parsley and toss to coat. Serve at room temperature or chilled. Store leftovers in an airtight container in the refrigerator for up to 4 days.

MAKE-AHEAD TIP: Cook the carrots and toss with the spices, schug, and lemon juice. Dress with the olive oil and parsley right before serving.

COOKING TIP: Some grocery stores sell presliced carrot rounds, but I actually don't recommend them for this recipe—they're usually sliced too thin and will fall apart when you boil them. Stick to whole carrots instead.

Simple Overnight Marinated Broccoli

GLUTEN-FREE, GREAT FOR SHABBAT,
PAREVE, VEGETARIAN

SERVES 4 • PREP TIME: 15 MINUTES, PLUS OVERNIGHT TO MARINATE

This might be the easiest, most hands-off recipe in this entire book. The broccoli is marinated overnight in a tangy mustard-and-vinegar dressing that softens it up while preserving all the nutrients that would otherwise be lost during cooking. This recipe works just as well with a mixture of cauliflower and broccoli florets. Since it's meant to be eaten cold or at room temperature, this is a perfect side dish to make ahead for Shabbat lunch.

2 garlic cloves, minced

1 teaspoon sea salt

¼ teaspoon freshly ground black pepper

1 tablespoon Dijon mustard

3 tablespoons light brown sugar

¼ cup avocado oil

¼ cup apple cider vinegar

2 (12-ounce) packages raw broccoli florets

1. In a large zip-top bag, combine the garlic, salt, pepper, mustard, brown sugar, avocado oil, and vinegar. Seal the bag and squeeze it to ensure the ingredients are mixed together.

2. Add the broccoli to the bag, reseal it, and shake it to ensure the broccoli is coated in the marinade. Place in the refrigerator to marinate overnight.

3. Serve the next day, chilled or at room temperature. Store leftovers in an airtight container in the refrigerator for up to 3 days.

INGREDIENT TIP: If you're in a rush, you can technically marinate the broccoli in 2 to 3 hours. Just know that time is your friend in this recipe—it will always taste better the next day.

Roasted Vegetable Soup 54

CHAPTER 4

Soups and Stews

A good soup or stew is a staple element for any Shabbat or holiday meal, but soups are also fantastic, often-easy options for cooking on busy weeknights. The soups and stews in this chapter take advantage of pantry staples as well as fresh vegetables and a variety of proteins. The recipes range from light, blended options, like Zucchini Dill Soup and Creamy Carrot Soup, to heartier ones that can stand on their own as main courses, like Shawarma-Spiced Lamb and Vegetable Stew and Mushroom, Barley, and Kale Soup. Of course, I couldn't write this chapter without including my personal take on the hall-of-famer of Jewish soups, Classic Chicken Soup.

Classic Chicken Soup

GLUTEN-FREE, GREAT FOR SHABBAT, WEEKEND

SERVES 4 TO 6 • PREP TIME: 30 MINUTES / COOK TIME: 1 HOUR 30 MINUTES

Every household needs a tried-and-true recipe for chicken soup. I always have some of this soup on standby in the freezer for when my kids are under the weather (after all, everything's better with Mom's chicken soup). This soup is a classic staple course for Shabbat and holiday meals. If you have a small amount left over, strain it and freeze in an ice cube tray to use as broth. See the cooking tip for making clear chicken soup.

1 whole chicken (about 3½ pounds)

2 onions, quartered

1 turnip, peeled and quartered

3 carrots, halved

3 celery stalks, halved

6 parsnips, peeled and halved

1 celery root, peeled and quartered

1 bunch dill

1 bunch parsley

2 tablespoons ground turmeric

1 teaspoon sea salt

1. Place the whole chicken in a large soup pot with a lid. Add the onions, turnip, carrots, celery, parsnips, celery root, dill, parsley, turmeric, and salt. Fill the pot with water so the water comes just to the top of the ingredients but doesn't cover them entirely.

2. Set the pot over medium-high heat and bring the water to a boil. Once boiling, cover, reduce the heat to low, and simmer for 1 hour 30 minutes, or until the internal temperature of the chicken reaches 165°F.

3. **For broth:** To use this as broth, strain the cooking liquid into a container. Discard the vegetables and save the cooked chicken for another use.
   For chicken soup: Transfer the chicken to a cutting board and pull the meat off the bone into bite-size pieces. Scoop the vegetables and herbs from the soup pot, chop the ones you want in the soup, and discard the rest. Return the chicken and chopped vegetables to the soup pot.

4. Serve the broth or soup hot. Store leftovers in an airtight container in the refrigerator for up to 2 days, or in the freezer for up to 3 months.

COOKING TIP: If you like clear chicken soup, instead of scooping out the vegetables (see step 3), strain everything through a fine-mesh sieve. Return the strained soup to the pot and then add any sliced vegetables or chicken back in. For ultra-clear chicken broth, freeze or refrigerate the strained broth—the fat will solidify at the top and you can scrape it off before reheating.

Blended Chickpea Soup

GLUTEN-FREE, PAREVE, VEGETARIAN, WEEKNIGHT

SERVES 4 • PREP TIME: 15 MINUTES / COOK TIME: 15 MINUTES

This creamy blended chickpea soup can be thrown together in minutes using pantry staples you likely already have on hand. It's a true standby that I often turn to on busy weeknights when it feels like there's nothing to eat. Once garnished with sunflower seeds (or chopped scallions), this soup looks and feels like a fancy restaurant appetizer. For added spice, stir in 1 to 2 teaspoons of Israeli Schug (page 125) just before serving.

2 (15-ounce) cans chickpeas, drained and rinsed

1 cup salsa of your choice (see Variation)

1 teaspoon ground cumin

1 teaspoon sea salt

½ teaspoon freshly ground black pepper

2 cups vegetable broth

1 (13-ounce) can full-fat coconut milk

Juice of 1 lime

¼ cup sunflower seeds, for garnish

1. In a blender, combine the chickpeas, salsa, cumin, salt, and pepper. Blend until smooth, then pour into a medium saucepan.

2. Add the broth, coconut milk, and lime juice to the pan and heat over medium-low heat for about 10 minutes to heat the soup through.

3. Serve the soup hot, garnished with the sunflower seeds. Store leftovers in an airtight container in the refrigerator for up to 2 days, or in the freezer for up to 3 months.

VARIATION TIP: The beauty of this recipe is that any jarred salsa will work—try different kinds to switch up the flavors. I recently made this with a mango salsa because it was all I had, and it came out fantastic.

INGREDIENT TIP: If you don't have chickpeas, you can make this soup with black, white, or kidney beans.

Roasted Vegetable Soup

GLUTEN-FREE, PAREVE, VEGETARIAN, WEEKNIGHT

SERVES 4 • PREP TIME: 15 MINUTES / COOK TIME: 1 HOUR

This could really be called use-up-the-leftovers soup, since you can use any vegetables to make it. I frequently make this soup with roasted vegetables left over from Shabbat. If you're using leftover cooked vegetables, skip the roasting step; the rest of the recipe stays the same. You can also add leftover meat—just shred it and add it to the pot after you add the spices. If I'm serving this soup as a main dish, I add a can of chickpeas or other beans when I add the vegetables and canned tomatoes. Serve the soup with toasted bread or mixed greens on the side.

2 onions, sliced

2 bell peppers (red, yellow, orange), sliced

1 (12-ounce) package cauliflower florets

2 tablespoons olive oil

1 (14.5-ounce) can diced tomatoes, undrained

6 cups vegetable broth

¼ cup Thai sweet chili sauce

½ teaspoon sea salt

¼ teaspoon freshly ground black pepper

1 teaspoon dried oregano

1. Preheat the oven to 400°F. Line a baking sheet with parchment paper.

2. Spread the onions, bell peppers, and cauliflower in a single layer on the prepared pan and toss with the olive oil. Roast for 25 minutes, or until tender and slightly browned.

3. Transfer the roasted vegetables to a large soup pot. Add the diced tomatoes and their juices, the broth, sweet chili sauce, salt, black pepper, and oregano. Bring the mixture to a boil over medium-high heat. Cover, reduce the heat to low, and simmer for 30 minutes, or until thickened.

4. Serve the soup hot. Store leftovers in an airtight container in the refrigerator for up to 2 days, or in the freezer for up to 3 months.

COOKING TIP: When roasting, it's always important to spread the vegetables in a single layer—if you crowd the pan, they'll end up steaming instead of roasting. If you don't have a large enough pan, use two smaller ones instead.

Shawarma-Spiced Lamb and Vegetable Stew

GREAT FOR SHABBAT, WEEKEND

SERVES 4 TO 6 • PREP TIME: 20 MINUTES / COOK TIME: 2 HOURS

This delicious, hearty stew stands on its own as a complete Shabbat meal. Even those who tend to avoid lamb will like this melt-in-your-mouth dish. The fat from the lamb flavors the vegetables, while the vegetables release liquid to create a thick sauce that braises the lamb, making it ultra tender. Don't be intimidated by the long cook time: Once you add the ingredients, you can leave it alone—it practically cooks itself!

2 pounds lamb stew meat, cubed

1 teaspoon sea salt

1 teaspoon freshly ground black pepper

1 teaspoon shawarma spice blend

2 small eggplants, sliced into ½-inch-thick rounds

2 small onions, sliced into thin rounds

3 tomatoes, sliced into thin rounds

4 potatoes, sliced into thin rounds

1 (12-ounce) bottle dark beer, such as stout or porter

1. In a large pot or Dutch oven, combine the lamb, salt, pepper, and shawarma spice blend. Layer the vegetables flat over the lamb in concentric circles, working one vegetable at a time, in this order: eggplant, onions, tomatoes, potatoes. Pour the beer over the entire mixture.

2. Cover the pot and cook over low heat for 2 hours, or until the lamb is tender and has reached an internal temperature of 145°F.

3. Serve the stew hot. Store leftovers in an airtight container in the refrigerator for up to 3 days.

VARIATION TIP: For a gluten-free version, use 1½ cups red wine in place of the beer.

Curried Lentil Soup

GLUTEN-FREE, PAREVE, VEGETARIAN, WEEKNIGHT

SERVES 4 TO 6 • PREP TIME: 15 MINUTES / COOK TIME: 50 MINUTES

Lentil soup is an easy, healthy, and delicious way to add fiber to your diet. A single serving of this lentil soup has about 12 grams of fiber, which is a third of the recommended daily amount. This version, spiced with curry, cumin, and other seasonings, is filling enough to be a meal on its own, and reheats perfectly for leftovers the next day. I often make a double batch and freeze half to reheat for a quick lunch or dinner.

2 tablespoons avocado oil

2 large onions, finely diced

3 celery stalks, finely diced

2 carrots, finely diced

2 teaspoons ground cumin

1 teaspoon curry powder

1 teaspoon sea salt

½ teaspoon freshly ground black pepper

½ teaspoon dried oregano

3 garlic cloves, minced

1 (16-ounce) package dried lentils (see Tip)

1 (28-ounce) can diced tomatoes, undrained

2 cups baby spinach

Juice of ½ lemon

1. In a large soup pot, heat the avocado oil over medium-high heat. Once hot, add the onions, celery, and carrots and cook, stirring occasionally, for 10 minutes, or until softened.

2. Add the cumin, curry powder, salt, pepper, oregano, and garlic to the pot and stir to coat the vegetables. Cook, stirring occasionally, for 3 to 5 minutes, until very fragrant.

3. Stir in the lentils and cook for 5 minutes—they should start to smell earthy and almost toasty.

4. Stir in the diced tomatoes and their juices. Add enough water to the pot to just cover all of the ingredients. Bring the soup to a simmer, then cover, reduce the heat to low, and cook for 30 more minutes.

5. Remove the soup from the heat, add the spinach and lemon juice, and stir to wilt the spinach. Serve hot. Store leftovers in an airtight container in the refrigerator for up to 2 days, or in the freezer for up to 4 months.

INGREDIENT TIP: You can use any type of lentil in this soup—green, black, red, or mixed versions will all work, though the texture of the soup will vary. Note that if you use red lentils, the consistency will be more similar to that of a thick blended soup, since red lentils are smaller and break down more easily.

Zucchini Dill Soup

GLUTEN-FREE, PAREVE, VEGETARIAN, WEEKNIGHT

SERVES 4 • PREP TIME: 15 MINUTES / COOK TIME: 30 MINUTES

I usually make this soup in the summer, when zucchini is at peak season, but it's delicious any time of year. Zucchini provides a delicious, light base for this soup, and the dill adds a bright, fresh flavor. Feel free to experiment by adding different herbs instead of or in addition to the dill—cilantro and mint would both offer great complementary flavors.

2 tablespoons avocado oil

2 onions, coarsely chopped

2 celery stalks, coarsely chopped

2 carrots, coarsely chopped

1 teaspoon sea salt

2 garlic cloves, minced

6 zucchini, sliced into rounds

2 cups stemmed and coarsely chopped kale leaves

½ bunch dill, rough stems discarded

Juice of ½ lemon

½ teaspoon freshly ground black pepper

1. In a large pot, heat the avocado oil over medium heat. Once hot, add the onions, celery, carrots, and salt and sauté, stirring occasionally, for 10 minutes, or until the vegetables are somewhat tender.

2. Add the garlic and sauté for 5 minutes, or until the garlic is fragrant and the vegetables are softened.

3. Add the zucchini and cook, stirring occasionally, for 5 minutes, or until translucent and starting to brown.

4. Add enough water to cover the vegetables and bring to a boil. Once boiling, cover, reduce the heat to medium-low, and simmer for 15 minutes.

5. Remove the pot from the heat and puree the mixture with an immersion blender until smooth. Add the kale and puree until smooth. Finally, add the dill, lemon juice, and pepper and puree one final time until completely smooth.

6. Serve the soup hot. Store leftovers in an airtight container in the refrigerator for up to 2 days, or in the freezer for up to 3 months.

Mushroom, Barley, and Kale Soup

GREAT FOR SHABBAT, PAREVE,
VEGETARIAN, WEEKNIGHT

SERVES 4 • PREP TIME: 10 MINUTES / COOK TIME: 40 MINUTES

As a kid, beef barley soup was one of my favorite foods. This recipe is a healthy, vegetarian, and just-as-enjoyable re-creation of that childhood favorite. The mushrooms and kale give the soup a hearty, well-rounded, earthy quality, making it an ideal comfort-food meal. This recipe is more than easy enough for a weeknight dinner, but also elegant enough to serve as a first course for a Shabbat or holiday meal.

½ cup pearl barley

1 bay leaf

5 cups water

1 tablespoon avocado oil

1 large onion, finely diced

2 (8-ounce) packages mushrooms, sliced

2 garlic cloves, minced

1 (14.5-ounce) can diced tomatoes, undrained

1 teaspoon dried dill or oregano

1 teaspoon sea salt

½ teaspoon freshly ground black pepper

2 cups chopped kale leaves

1. In a large soup pot, combine the barley, bay leaf, and water. Bring to a boil over high heat, then cover, reduce the heat to low, and simmer for 25 minutes.

2. Meanwhile, in a medium skillet, heat the avocado oil over medium heat. Once hot, add the onion, mushrooms, and garlic. Sauté, stirring often, for 10 minutes, until softened.

3. After the barley has been cooking for 25 minutes, discard the bay leaf and transfer the onion-mushroom mixture to the soup pot. Add the canned tomatoes and their juices, the dill, salt, and pepper. Stir to incorporate and bring the mixture to a boil. Once boiling, add the kale, then reduce the heat to low and simmer for 3 to 5 minutes to cook the kale through (it should turn bright green).

4. Serve the soup hot. Store leftovers in an airtight container in the refrigerator for up to 3 days, or in the freezer for up to 3 months.

VARIATION TIP: For a gluten-free soup, you can use precooked brown rice or quinoa in place of the barley. Skip step 1 and combine about 1½ cups cooked rice or quinoa, 3½ cups water, and the bay leaf in a soup pot, then add the onion-mushroom mixture and proceed as directed. Discard the bay leaf before serving.

Creamy Carrot Soup

GLUTEN-FREE, GREAT FOR SHABBAT,
PAREVE, VEGETARIAN, WEEKNIGHT

SERVES 4 • PREP TIME: 20 MINUTES / COOK TIME: 25 MINUTES

This deceptively simple but showstopping carrot soup is more than the sum of its parts. I tried a dairy version of this soup at my friend's house and immediately created this pareve adaptation to serve on Shabbat and other holidays. It makes an ideal addition to a Rosh Hashanah, Sukkot, or Simchat Torah meal. Serve with a side salad dressed with Pareve Caesar Dressing (page 123). If serving at a dairy meal, swap out the coconut cream for sour cream or plain Greek yogurt.

2 pounds carrots, coarsely chopped

1 small sweet potato, peeled and coarsely chopped

4 cups vegetable broth

1 teaspoon sea salt

2 tablespoons avocado oil

1 onion, coarsely chopped

2 garlic cloves, finely chopped

½ cup blanched or slivered almonds

1 cup coconut cream

¼ teaspoon dried parsley

¼ teaspoon ground nutmeg

¼ teaspoon ground cinnamon

1. In a large soup pot, combine the carrots, sweet potato, broth, and salt. Bring to a boil over medium-high heat, then cover and simmer for 15 minutes, or until the carrots and sweet potato are fork-tender.

2. Meanwhile, in a medium skillet, heat the avocado oil over medium heat. Once hot, add the onion, garlic, and almonds and sauté for 5 minutes, or until softened and fragrant. Remove from the heat.

3. Stir the onion-almond mixture into the soup pot. Using an immersion blender, puree the mixture until smooth and well blended.

4. Reduce the heat to medium-low and whisk in the coconut cream, parsley, nutmeg, and cinnamon. Cook for 3 to 5 minutes more, until heated through.

5. Serve the soup hot. Store leftovers in an airtight container in the refrigerator for up to 3 days, or in the freezer for up to 3 months.

VARIATION TIP: This soup is also delicious with homemade challah croutons. Slice leftover challah into cubes, toss with a few tablespoons of olive oil, and bake at 375°F for 15 minutes, or until golden brown. Serve on top of the soup.

Vegetarian "Crab" Cakes 75

CHAPTER 5

Dairy, Fish, and Veggie Mains

When considering classic Jewish main courses, meat-centric dishes like brisket, cholent, and roast chicken usually come to mind first. While those are all fantastic, there's a whole other spectrum of vegetarian, fish, and dairy recipes that stand on their own as main-course meals. These recipes are especially important for kosher households—and as a nutritionist, you don't have to tell me twice that not every meal has to be a meat meal. This chapter features a wide range of meatless recipes, from the fancy (Honey-Roasted Onion and Apple Tart) to the quick-and-easy (Crispy Roasted Tofu and Vegetables) to adaptations of the traditional (Super-Simple Baked Gefilte Fish).

Baked Macaroni and Cheese with Broccoli

VEGETARIAN, WEEKNIGHT

SERVES 4 TO 6 • PREP TIME: 25 MINUTES / COOK TIME: 25 MINUTES

Who doesn't love old-fashioned macaroni and cheese? This recipe already tastes good before it goes in the oven, but the extra step of baking it is well worth the effort, resulting in a crunchy crust on the top and a stronger, better-developed flavor inside. I initially included the broccoli just to sneak in a serving of vegetables, but I found that it helped to round out the meal, giving the sauce a smoother consistency. Try serving a simple green salad dressed with Pareve Caesar Dressing (page 123).

Cooking spray

1 (16-ounce) package fusilli pasta

2 tablespoons potato starch

1 teaspoon mustard powder

1¼ teaspoons freshly ground black pepper

1 teaspoon sea salt

2 cups milk

2 tablespoons unsalted butter

8 ounces cheddar cheese, shredded

8 ounces mozzarella cheese, shredded

1 (12-ounce) package frozen broccoli, thawed

½ cup fine dried bread crumbs

1. Preheat the oven to 375°F. Mist a 9-by-13-inch glass baking dish with cooking spray.

2. Cook the pasta according to the package directions. Drain and set aside.

3. Meanwhile, in a large pot, mix together the potato starch, mustard powder, pepper, and salt. Stir in the milk and add the butter. Bring the mixture to a boil over medium heat, stirring often. Allow the mixture to boil for 1 minute, stirring continuously to prevent scorching.

4. After 1 minute, turn off the heat and immediately add the cheddar and mozzarella and stir vigorously to incorporate. Add the drained pasta and broccoli and stir to coat thoroughly in the cheese sauce.

5. Pour the contents of the pot into the prepared baking dish. Top evenly with the bread crumbs.

6. Bake the macaroni and cheese for 25 minutes, or until the bread crumbs are golden brown on top. Serve hot. Store leftovers in an airtight container in the refrigerator for up to 3 days.

Risotto with Carrots and Goat Cheese

VEGETARIAN, WEEKNIGHT

SERVES 4 • PREP TIME: 10 MINUTES / COOK TIME: 30 MINUTES

I used to think risotto was the kind of dish you could only order at a restaurant because it was too complicated to make at home. I'm happy to say I was mistaken. This is my recipe for at-home risotto, and I promise it's as easy as it is creamy and delicious. Carrots, goat cheese, and lemon might sound like an unusual flavor combination on paper, but try this recipe and see for yourself—it's an absolute taste sensation.

5 cups vegetable broth

2 (8-ounce) packages shredded carrots

2 tablespoons olive oil

2 onions, finely diced

3 cups Arborio rice

1 teaspoon dried parsley

Juice of 2 lemons

1 cup crumbled goat cheese

1. In a medium pot, combine the broth and carrots. Set the pot over medium heat to keep the broth hot throughout the cooking process, as you'll slowly add it to the risotto.

2. In a large, deep saucepan, heat the olive oil over medium heat. Once hot, add the onions and sauté for about 5 minutes, until softened. Stir the rice into the onions with a wooden spoon to coat with the oil. Stir in the parsley.

3. Working one ladleful at a time, ladle the hot carrot-broth mixture into the rice and stir until incorporated. Allow the rice to absorb all of the liquid—it should take a few minutes.

4. Once the liquid has been absorbed, add another ladleful of carrots and broth to the rice. Continue this way, making sure to wait until all the liquid has been absorbed before you add another ladleful of broth. Keep going until no broth is left—it should take about 20 minutes. When finished, the risotto should be creamy, with no excess liquid remaining.

5. Remove the risotto from the heat. Stir in the lemon juice and goat cheese and serve hot. Store leftovers in an airtight container in the refrigerator for up to 2 days.

Honey-Roasted Onion and Apple Tart

GREAT FOR SHABBAT, VEGETARIAN, WEEKEND

SERVES 4 TO 6 • PREP TIME: 45 MINUTES / COOK TIME: 1 HOUR 30 MINUTES

This festive tart is a great addition to a Yom Tov (holiday) dairy lunch or a weekend brunch, and it's perfect for Rosh Hashanah, when we eat apples and honey. I use Vidalia onions for their milder flavor—if you use another type of onion, the flavor will not be as delicate. Caramelizing the onions brings out their sweetness, making them a perfect match for apples and sour cream. Kids and adults alike will enjoy this sophisticated, grown-up "pizza" on a flaky puff pastry base.

¼ cup honey

¼ cup white wine

2 tablespoons avocado oil

3 Vidalia onions, thinly sliced

2 sheets store-bought frozen puff pastry, thawed

1 cup sour cream

1 teaspoon dried thyme

½ teaspoon sea salt

⅛ teaspoon ground cinnamon

3 apples, peeled, cored, and sliced

1. Preheat the oven to 375°F. Line two baking sheets with parchment paper.

2. In a medium bowl, combine the honey, wine, and avocado oil. Add the onions and toss to coat.

3. Spread the onions in a single layer on the one of the prepared pans. Roast for 30 minutes, or until browned and caramelized.

4. Meanwhile, unroll the puff pastry sheets and set them side by side on the second prepared baking sheet. Overlap the pastry just slightly in the middle and lightly roll with a rolling pin to flatten the seam and make one large sheet of pastry. Using your fingers, crimp the edges of the puff pastry to form a rim. Place in the refrigerator to keep chilled.

5. Once the onions are done, remove them from the oven and set aside to cool. Increase the oven temperature to 400°F.

6. Meanwhile, in a small bowl, mix together the sour cream, thyme, salt, and cinnamon.

7. Remove the chilled puff pastry from the refrigerator. Using a spatula, spread the sour cream mixture in an even layer across the puff pastry, avoiding the rim. Arrange the apples in a single layer over the sour cream mixture. Top the apples evenly with the cooled caramelized onions.

8. Bake the tart for 25 minutes, or until the apples are soft and the pastry is golden brown.

9. Cut the tart into squares and serve hot. Store leftovers in an airtight container in the refrigerator for 1 to 2 days. Reheat in the microwave for 1 to 2 minutes or in a 300°F oven for 20 to 30 minutes.

VARIATION TIP: To make a pareve tart, use plain (unsweetened) nondairy yogurt in place of the sour cream.

Chili-Marinated Salmon

GLUTEN-FREE, GREAT FOR SHABBAT, PAREVE

SERVES 4 TO 6 • PREP TIME: 20 MINUTES, PLUS OVERNIGHT
TO MARINATE / COOK TIME: 1 HOUR

This recipe is an adaptation of my cousin's recipe for ketchup-marinated salmon. My daughter isn't a fan of ketchup, so I thought I'd try using Thai sweet chili sauce instead. The result was a success, giving the salmon an amazing sweet-and-sour taste. This salmon is a great make-ahead recipe to serve as a Friday-night appetizer or as a main course for Shabbat lunch. I often make this dish for 3-day Yom Tov holidays, since it keeps for a good 5 days in the refrigerator.

1½ cups coconut sugar, divided

2 pounds salmon fillets, cut into 3-ounce portions

1 cup distilled white vinegar

1 cup Thai sweet chili sauce

1 cup water

2 red onions, thinly sliced

1. Fill a large pot halfway with water and stir in ½ cup of the sugar. Bring to a boil over high heat, stirring to dissolve the sugar.

2. Place the salmon fillets into the boiling water. Immediately cover the pot with a lid and turn off the heat. Let stand for 1 hour to poach.

3. Meanwhile, in a large bowl, mix together the remaining 1 cup sugar, the vinegar, chili sauce, and water. Set aside while the salmon finishes poaching.

4. Remove the poached salmon from the pot and transfer it to the bowl with the chili sauce mixture. Fold gently to coat, then scatter the onions on top.

5. Cover the bowl and marinate in the refrigerator overnight.

6. The next day, serve the salmon chilled. Store leftovers in an airtight container in the refrigerator for up to 5 days.

VARIATION TIP: If you have low spice tolerance, you can do my cousin's version of this recipe—use the same amount of ketchup in place of the sweet chili sauce.

For David, Danielle, Emily, Samantha,
and Hannah: You all are my biggest
fans and my best critics!

Super-Simple Baked Gefilte Fish

GREAT FOR SHABBAT, PAREVE

SERVES 4 TO 6 • PREP TIME: 10 MINUTES, PLUS 20 MINUTES TO COOL /
COOK TIME: 1 HOUR 30 MINUTES

Gefilte fish can be a polarizing food—many people either love it or hate it. I'd actually never tried gefilte fish until my husband asked me if I'd consider making it, and that's how this dish was born. This modern take on old-school gefilte fish is a challenge to that claim, tempting even those who insist gefilte fish is just not for them. It looks quite striking when you slice it, making it a festive addition to Shabbat or holiday meals.

2 tablespoons avocado oil

1 sweet onion, thinly sliced

1 (20- or 22-ounce) loaf frozen gefilte fish

1 cup Homemade Savory Marinara Sauce (page 124) or store-bought spicy marinara

4 to 6 lettuce leaves, for garnish

1. Preheat the oven to 350°F.

2. Grease a 9-inch square baking dish with the avocado oil. Spread the onion in an even layer over the bottom of the prepared baking dish.

3. Lay the gefilte fish loaf whole on top of the onion. Pour the marinara sauce over the loaf to coat it.

4. Bake the fish, uncovered, for 1½ hours. Let cool for at least 20 minutes before slicing.

5. Once cool enough to slice without falling apart, cut the loaf into 1-inch-thick slices. Arrange them on a platter of lettuce leaves along with the onion from the baking dish and refrigerate until ready to serve. Serve chilled. Store leftovers in an airtight container in the refrigerator for up to 4 days.

MAKE-AHEAD TIP: If you're making the gefilte fish ahead of time, refrigerate the unsliced loaf in the baking dish, covered. Slice and plate just before serving.

One-Pot Braised Fish and Vegetables

GLUTEN-FREE, PAREVE, WEEKNIGHT

SERVES 4 TO 6 • PREP TIME: 20 MINUTES / COOK TIME: 45 MINUTES

My mom is a great cook, and we often trade recipes back and forth. She made this recipe for the first time one night and immediately called me afterward to tell me I had to make it. I did, and the result was an absolutely crave-worthy dish. It's a true all-in-one meal, with protein, veggies, and starch all cooked together in a single pot. You can use any type of lean white fish—my personal favorite is red snapper.

2 tablespoons olive oil

1 onion, cubed

2 garlic cloves, minced

1 red bell pepper, cut into large squares

2 portobello mushroom caps, sliced

2 tomatoes, cubed

6 red potatoes, cubed

2 tablespoons tomato paste

1 teaspoon sea salt

½ teaspoon freshly ground black pepper

1 teaspoon dried oregano

¼ cup red wine

4 cups vegetable broth

2 pounds white-fleshed fish fillets, cut into bite-size pieces

1. Preheat the oven to 400°F.

2. In a large Dutch oven (or other large ovenproof pot), heat the olive oil over medium heat. Once hot, add the onion and sauté for about 10 minutes, until browned.

3. Add the garlic, bell pepper, mushrooms, tomatoes, and potatoes and sauté, stirring often, for about 15 minutes, until the vegetables are tender and the potatoes start to turn golden brown.

4. Stir in the tomato paste, then stir in the salt, black pepper, and oregano. Add the wine and cook, stirring occasionally and using a wooden spoon to loosen any stuck bits from the bottom of the pan, for 5 minutes. Add the broth and mix it into the sauce.

5. Add the fish and spoon some of the brothy sauce on top to cover it partially. Transfer the entire pot, uncovered, to the oven and bake for 30 minutes.

6. Remove the pot from the oven and serve the fish hot, with extra sauce spooned over the top.

Spiced Tilapia Braised with Chickpeas

GLUTEN-FREE, GREAT FOR SHABBAT, PAREVE

SERVES 4 • PREP TIME: 15 MINUTES / COOK TIME: 1 HOUR

This recipe is among the most-requested dinners at my house. Braising might not be the most well-known method of cooking fish, but it's popular in Mediterranean and Israeli cooking, which is the basis for this recipe. The technique works wonders, making the tilapia ultra-flaky and tender so it can absorb the flavors of the spices. The chickpeas add a heartiness to the dish, not to mention plenty of protein.

2 tablespoons avocado oil

1 onion, coarsely chopped

6 garlic cloves, minced

2 tomatoes, coarsely chopped

1 teaspoon ground cumin

1 teaspoon curry powder

1 teaspoon sea salt

½ teaspoon freshly ground black pepper

1 teaspoon Israeli Schug (page 125) or any store-bought schug

1 (15-ounce) can chickpeas, drained and rinsed

2 pounds tilapia fillets, cut into 3-ounce portions

1 cup tomato sauce

1. In a large skillet, heat the avocado oil over medium heat. Once hot, add the onion, garlic, tomatoes, cumin, curry powder, salt, pepper, and schug. Sauté for 5 minutes, stirring often to prevent sticking.

2. Add the chickpeas and fish fillets to the skillet, then pour the tomato sauce over the top. Add enough water to the pan to come just to the top of the fish without covering it. Bring the mixture to a boil, then cover, reduce the heat to low, and simmer for 45 minutes, or until the fish is tender and flaky.

3. Serve hot, with extra sauce spooned over the top.

VARIATION TIP: This flavor combination also works wonderfully with the same amount of salmon.

Sesame-Ginger Soba Noodles

GREAT FOR SHABBAT, PAREVE,
VEGETARIAN, WEEKNIGHT

SERVES 4 • PREP TIME: 15 MINUTES / COOK TIME: 20 MINUTES

This recipe is my lighter take on noodles in peanut sauce. The soba noodles offer a nice chewy texture that pairs well with the tangy sauce. This is a great dish for Shabbat because it's meant to be eaten cold or at room temperature. Plus, you can make the components a day ahead and assemble the dish just before serving (see the make-ahead tip after the recipe).

For the sesame-ginger sauce

¼ cup rice vinegar

Juice of ½ lemon

1 teaspoon soy sauce

2 tablespoons white miso paste

1 tablespoon honey

1 (½-inch) piece fresh ginger, peeled and grated

½ teaspoon freshly ground black pepper

1 tablespoon avocado oil

1 tablespoon toasted sesame oil

For the noodle bowls

1 (14-ounce) package soba noodles

1 head broccoli, cut into florets

4 scallions, sliced

1 (14-ounce) can sliced bamboo shoots, drained

1 (8-ounce) can sliced water chestnuts, drained

2 tablespoons sesame seeds, for garnish

1. **To make the sesame-ginger sauce:** In a large bowl, whisk together the vinegar, lemon juice, soy sauce, miso, honey, ginger, and pepper. Add the avocado oil and sesame oil and whisk vigorously to combine. Set aside.

2. **To make the noodle bowls:** Cook the soba noodles according to the package directions. Drain and set aside to cool.

3. Meanwhile, boil a kettle of water and put the broccoli in a large heatproof bowl. Once the water is boiling, pour it over the broccoli. Let stand for 5 minutes, then drain the broccoli and set aside to cool.

4. Just before serving, add the soba noodles to the bowl of sesame-ginger sauce and toss to combine. Add the blanched broccoli, scallions, bamboo shoots, and water chestnuts and toss to incorporate.

5. Serve in bowls chilled or at room temperature, garnished with the sesame seeds.

MAKE-AHEAD TIP: The sesame-ginger sauce can be prepared up to 3 days in advance, and the soba noodles and broccoli up to 1 day in advance. Store the noodles, broccoli, and dressing separately until just before serving.

Mashed Black Bean Tacos

GLUTEN-FREE, PAREVE, VEGETARIAN, WEEKNIGHT

SERVES 4 • PREP TIME: 30 MINUTES / COOK TIME: 5 MINUTES

These super-easy vegetarian tacos are a terrific pantry dinner for a busy week-night. They're satisfyingly meaty—without any actual meat, of course—and tend to be a crowd-pleaser since everyone can choose their own toppings. Some of my favorite toppings are vegan sour cream, spicy mayonnaise, diced avocado, salsa, coleslaw, and Barbecue Ranch Sauce (page 116).

1 tablespoon tomato paste

2 tablespoons hot sauce of your choice (I like Sriracha)

1 tablespoon Dijon mustard

2 tablespoons apple cider vinegar

2 (15-ounce) cans black beans, drained and liquid reserved, divided

2 teaspoons olive oil

1 small onion, chopped

3 garlic cloves, minced

1 carrot, chopped

1 celery stalk, chopped

½ teaspoon sea salt

½ teaspoon freshly ground black pepper

8 to 12 (6-inch) corn tortillas or hard taco shells

Toppings of your choice, for serving

1. In a small bowl, whisk together the tomato paste, hot sauce, mustard, vinegar, and ¼ cup of the reserved black bean liquid. (Hold on to the rest of the bean liquid for later.)

2. In a separate small bowl, mash ½ cup of the black beans. Add the seasoned black bean liquid to the mashed beans and stir to incorporate. Set aside.

3. In a large skillet, heat the olive oil over medium heat. Once hot, add the onion, garlic, carrot, and celery and sauté for about 5 minutes, or until the vegetables are softened.

4. Add the mashed bean mixture and the remaining black beans. Cook, stirring often, for about 1 minute, until the mixture is heated through. If the mixture seems dry or the beans are sticking, add more of the reserved bean liquid a tablespoon at a time until it reaches your desired consistency.

5. Remove the bean mixture from the heat and season with the salt and pepper.

6. To serve, spoon the bean filling into corn tortillas or taco shells and add the toppings of your choice. Store any leftover bean filling in an airtight container in the refrigerator for up to 3 days.

Crispy Roasted Tofu and Vegetables

PAREVE, VEGETARIAN, WEEKNIGHT

SERVES 4 • PREP TIME: 15 MINUTES, PLUS 1 HOUR TO MARINATE /
COOK TIME: 25 MINUTES

Tofu is easy to make and wonderfully absorbent, taking on the flavors of whatever you cook it with. In this simple sheet pan recipe, the tofu is marinated and roasted alongside the vegetables, which gives it crispy edges but keeps the inside soft. Serve with rice or mixed greens dressed with Perfect Vinaigrette (page 120).

1 (12-ounce) package extra-firm tofu

2 red bell peppers, seeded and thinly sliced

1 red onion, cut into large squares

2 zucchini, cubed

1 (8-ounce) jar hoisin sauce

¼ cup toasted sesame oil

1. Cut the tofu into bite-size chunks and pat with a paper towel to remove excess moisture. Put the tofu in a medium bowl and set aside.

2. In a separate medium bowl, combine the bell peppers, onion, and zucchini.

3. In a small bowl, combine the hoisin sauce and sesame oil.

4. Add half of the sauce mixture to the bowl with the tofu and the other half to the bowl with the vegetables. Toss both mixtures to coat. Cover the bowls and marinate in the refrigerator for at least 1 hour.

5. Meanwhile, preheat the oven to 400°F. Line a baking sheet with parchment paper.

6. Spread the marinated tofu and the vegetables side-by-side on the prepared pan. Pour any remaining marinade from the bowls on top.

7. Roast for 25 minutes, or until tender and browned. Serve hot. Store leftovers in an airtight container in the refrigerator for up to 2 days.

MAKE-AHEAD TIP: To cut down on prep time, marinate the tofu and vegetables up to a day ahead, and keep them covered in the refrigerator until you're ready to roast them.

Vegetable Ragout Pasta

PAREVE, VEGETARIAN, WEEKNIGHT

SERVES 4 • PREP TIME: 15 MINUTES / COOK TIME: 20 MINUTES

This recipe comes to you from my daughter, who put it together one night using vegetables we had left over in the refrigerator. It was a hit, and it's now in our rotation of weeknight recipes. The vegetables are really the star of the show, but the white beans are key, adding creaminess to the veggies. The splash of balsamic vinegar and olives added right at the end make the dish pop, adding lovely depth of flavor.

1 (16-ounce) package penne pasta

2 tablespoons olive oil

1 onion, coarsely chopped

4 garlic cloves, minced

1 (4-ounce) package shiitake mush-
    rooms, sliced

2 plum tomatoes, coarsely chopped

½ teaspoon sea salt

½ teaspoon freshly ground black pepper

4 cups baby spinach

1 (15-ounce) can white beans, drained
    and rinsed

1 tablespoon balsamic vinegar

½ cup pitted olives of your choice

2 tablespoon chopped fresh parsley

1. Cook the pasta according to the package directions. Drain and set aside.

2. Meanwhile, in a large, deep skillet, heat the olive oil over medium heat. Once hot add the onion and sauté, stirring occasionally, for about 4 minutes, or until softened. Add the garlic and sauté for 1 minute more, until fragrant.

3. Add the mushrooms and tomatoes and sauté, stirring occasionally, for 5 minutes, or until softened. Season with the salt and pepper.

4. Add the spinach and stir until just wilted, about 1 minute. Add the beans and cook, stirring often, for 3 minutes to heat through. For a creamier ragout, use a wooden spoon to mash some of the beans.

5. Add the drained pasta to the pan and toss it with the vegetables to combine, ensuring it is thoroughly heated through. Add the vinegar and toss to incorporate.

6. Just before serving, transfer the pasta to a large bowl and toss with the olives and parsley. Serve hot, at room temperature, or chilled. Store leftovers in an airtight container in the refrigerator for up to 2 days.

Vegetarian "Crab" Cakes

GREAT FOR SHABBAT, PAREVE, VEGETARIAN, WEEKEND

MAKES 22 TO 24 PATTIES (SERVES 4 TO 6) • PREP TIME: 45 MINUTES /
COOK TIME: 30 MINUTES

These vegetarian "crab" cakes are so good, I actually find them a little bit addictive—luckily, this recipe makes a pretty big batch. They have a wonderful light-but-hearty texture and are packed with flavor, thanks in large part to hearts of palm, which when shredded take on a texture similar to crab. I suggest serving them over lettuce, drizzled with the barbecue ranch sauce for a great shellfish-free Shabbat or holiday appetizer.

Olive oil cooking spray

1 tablespoon olive oil

1 onion, coarsely chopped

2 red bell peppers, cut into large squares

2 garlic cloves, minced

2 (12-ounce) cans corn kernels, drained

2 (14-ounce) cans hearts of palm, drained

¼ cup chopped fresh cilantro

3 tablespoons Old Bay seasoning

1 cup fine dried bread crumbs

1 teaspoon Dijon mustard

¼ cup mayonnaise

4 to 6 lettuce leaves

½ cup Barbecue Ranch Sauce (page 116)

1. Preheat the oven to 400°F. Line two 18-by-13-inch baking sheets with parchment paper. Mist the paper lightly with cooking spray.

2. In a large skillet, combine the olive oil, onion, bell peppers, garlic, and corn. Sauté over medium heat for 5 minutes, until just softened.

3. Use an immersion blender to puree the corn mixture until it's just mashed. Remove the pan from the heat and set aside.

4. Grate or shred the hearts of palm into small pieces, about the size of peas. Transfer them to a large bowl and add the pureed corn mixture, cilantro, Old Bay, bread crumbs, mustard, and mayonnaise. Fold the mixture gently until fully incorporated.

5. Use your hands to form patties about 3 inches in diameter (you should get 22 to 24 patties). Place the patties on the prepared baking sheets spaced slightly apart.

6. Mist the top of each patty lightly with cooking spray. Bake for 30 minutes, or until the patties are golden brown on top.

CONTINUED

7. Divide the lettuce leaves among four to six plates and top each with 3 or 4 patties. Drizzle with the barbecue ranch sauce or serve it on the side for dipping.

MAKE-AHEAD TIP: To make this ahead, make and form the patties as directed and arrange them on a lined baking sheet, then refrigerate, covered, until ready to bake and serve—they'll keep for up to 2 days.

COOKING TIP: If you find the mixture is too soft and the patties are falling apart, refrigerate it for 10 to 20 minutes to firm it up before forming it into patties.

Rice Bowls with Avocado Dressing

GLUTEN-FREE, PAREVE, VEGETARIAN, WEEKEND

SERVES 4 • PREP TIME: 15 MINUTES / COOK TIME: 30 MINUTES

This vibrant rice bowl has it all: fluffy rice, fiber-packed vegetables, and a creamy dressing to top it off. Leftover rice bowls also make great, easy-to-pack school lunches, a favorite of my teenage daughters. I often make a double batch of the avocado dressing so I have extra to drizzle on simple green salads the following week. These rice bowls are also great topped with Barbecue Ranch Sauce (page 116) or Not-Your-Ordinary Pesto (page 117).

For the rice bowls

2 cups cooked brown rice

2 tablespoons olive oil

6 scallions, sliced

4 carrots, coarsely chopped

2 (15-ounce) cans chickpeas, drained and rinsed

2 cups baby spinach

½ teaspoon sea salt

½ teaspoon freshly ground black pepper

For the avocado dressing

1 avocado, halved and pitted

2 tablespoons olive oil

2 garlic cloves, minced

Juice of ½ lemon

2 tablespoons tahini

2 tablespoons water

½ teaspoon ground cumin

½ teaspoon sea salt

For assembly

¼ cup sunflower seeds, for garnish

1. **To make the rice bowls:** Place the rice in a large bowl and set aside.

2. In a large skillet, combine the olive oil, scallions, carrots, and chickpeas. Sauté over medium-high heat for 5 minutes, or until the carrots are slightly softened.

3. Add the spinach, salt, and pepper and cook for 3 minutes more, until the spinach wilts.

4. Add the sautéed vegetable mixture to the rice and toss to combine. Set aside.

5. **To make the avocado dressing:** Scoop the avocado flesh into a blender. Add the olive oil, garlic, lemon juice, tahini, water, cumin, and salt. Blend until smooth.

6. **To assemble:** Portion the rice-vegetable mixture into bowls and drizzle with the avocado dressing. Garnish with the sunflower seeds and serve immediately. Store leftover rice and dressing in separate airtight containers in the refrigerator for up to 3 days.

Grandma Dotty's Brisket 82

CHAPTER 6

Meat and Poultry

A lot of people, especially those new to cooking, are intimidated by meat dishes, under the assumption that they're too complicated to make. If this is you, I'm confident that this chapter will upend your expectations—these recipes are some of the easiest in this book. If you want to start simple, try the (three-ingredient!) Melt-in-Your-Mouth Ribs, the Oven-Roasted Chicken with Mushrooms and Tomatoes, or the Chicken and Cilantro Rice, each of which is assembled and cooked in a single dish using pantry staples. Some people are surprised to learn that many meat entrées can actually be frozen and reheated, and that's true for several recipes in this chapter, like Grandma Dotty's Brisket, Shredded Barbecue-Style Beef, and many other sauce-based dishes. You'll leave this chapter equipped with a diverse repertoire of easy, showstopping mains—so go forth and get cooking!

Grandma Dotty's Brisket

GREAT FOR SHABBAT, WEEKEND

SERVES 6 TO 8 • PREP TIME: 30 MINUTES, PLUS 1 HOUR TO REST /
COOK TIME: 3 HOURS 30 MINUTES

This fantastic brisket recipe is one I treasure—it's the same recipe my grandmother used to make when we visited her on holidays. Nowadays, my mother serves it when we come to her house. When I make the brisket myself, it sparks conversation with my kids about how recipes are like memories, passed down from generation to generation. Our recipe uses red wine, but if you're out, you can substitute beer—it's a different taste, but equally delicious.

1 teaspoon sea salt

1 teaspoon freshly ground black pepper

1 tablespoon paprika

2 tablespoons flour (or cornstarch, to make gluten-free)

5 pounds brisket

¼ cup avocado oil

8 onions, thinly sliced

2 cups beef broth

1 cup good-quality red wine

1. Preheat the oven to 375°F.

2. In a small bowl, combine the salt, pepper, paprika, and flour.

3. On a flat work surface (such as a cutting board), dredge the brisket on both sides with the seasoned flour.

4. Add the avocado oil to a large roasting pan and place on the stovetop over medium heat. Once the oil is hot, add the whole brisket to the pan.

5. Sear the brisket for 10 minutes on each side. Then transfer the brisket to a platter or cutting board to rest for a few minutes.

6. Meanwhile, add the onions to the roasting pan and sauté for 5 minutes, or until softened and browned, using a wooden spoon to loosen any stuck bits from the bottom of the pan.

7. Return the brisket and any accumulated drippings to the roasting pan, on top of the onions. Add the broth and wine. Bring the broth and wine to a boil, then turn off the heat and cover the pan with aluminum foil.

8. Transfer the pan to the oven and roast the brisket for 3 hours.

9. Remove the pan from the oven and transfer the brisket to a cutting board to rest for 1 hour.

10. Meanwhile, use an immersion blender to puree the onions and drippings directly in the roasting pan. Transfer the gravy to a serving dish and set aside.

11. After the brisket has rested, cut it into 1-inch-thick strips, slicing against the grain. Transfer to a serving dish and pour at least half of the gravy over the sliced brisket.

12. Serve the brisket with the remaining gravy on the side. Store leftover brisket and gravy in an airtight container in the refrigerator for up to 3 days, or in the freezer for up to 3 months.

MAKE-AHEAD TIP: This is a great dish to make in advance. It freezes extremely well, and the onion gravy keeps the brisket moist. Reheat on the stovetop over medium-low heat or in the oven at 325°F until heated through.

Shredded Barbecue-Style Beef

GLUTEN-FREE, GREAT FOR SHABBAT, WEEKEND, WEEKNIGHT

SERVES 12 TO 15 • PREP TIME: 15 MINUTES / COOK TIME: 4 HOURS

This slow-cooked, hands-off shredded beef recipe practically melts in your mouth. Serve it on a bun, in tacos, over rice, or with salad. To save even more time, you can use a bottle of store-bought barbecue sauce instead. It pairs wonderfully with Garlicky Eggplant Spread (page 118) and Red Pepper Spread (page 119). If you're making this recipe ahead to freeze, be sure to mix it with the sauce before freezing to ensure it stays moist.

For the beef

2 onions, thinly sliced

5 pounds California or brick roast

1 (2-ounce) packet onion soup mix

2 tablespoons soy sauce

1½ cups good-quality red wine (about ½ bottle)

For the sauce

1 cup ketchup

½ cup packed light brown sugar

1 teaspoon Dijon mustard

1 teaspoon distilled white vinegar

1. Preheat the oven to 300°F.

2. **To make the beef:** Put the onions in a large roasting pan. Place the roast on top of the onions. Sprinkle the onion soup mix over the meat and pour on the soy sauce and wine.

3. Cover the pan with aluminum foil and bake for 4 hours.

4. **To make the sauce:** In a large bowl, whisk together the ketchup, sugar, mustard, and vinegar. Set the sauce aside.

5. Remove the roast from the oven and transfer it to a cutting board. When cool enough to handle, shred the meat with two forks. Transfer the onions to the cutting board and coarsely chop them.

6. Add the shredded meat and chopped onions to the bowl with the sauce and stir to coat.

7. Serve hot. Store leftovers in an airtight container in the refrigerator for 2 to 3 days, or in the freezer for up to 1 month.

COOKING TIP: You can also make this recipe in a slow cooker: Throw the beef into the slow cooker in the late morning, set it on low for 8 hours, and it will be ready to shred, mix with sauce, and serve by dinnertime.

Pepper Steak and Vegetables with Peanut Sauce

GLUTEN-FREE, GREAT FOR SHABBAT, WEEKEND

SERVES 4 TO 6 • PREP TIME: 30 MINUTES / COOK TIME: 1 HOUR 30 MINUTES

In my opinion, braising is a vastly underused technique for cooking meat. It produces tender, flavor-packed results, and it can give even the toughest cuts of meat a melt-in-your-mouth texture. This recipe uses lean pepper steak, but lots of different cuts will work—you can try London broil, sirloin, or even cubed veal. This hearty dish is delicious on its own or served over a bowl of rice.

1½ cups peanut butter

3 cups water, divided

2 tablespoons peanut oil

4 pounds pepper steak, cut into strips

1 large onion, coarsely chopped

2 red bell peppers, coarsely chopped

4 garlic cloves, minced

1 teaspoon sea salt

1 teaspoon hot sauce of your choice

1 (14.5-ounce) can diced tomatoes, undrained

3 potatoes, peeled and finely diced

4 parsnips, peeled and cut into rounds

1 (8-ounce) package baby spinach

1. Preheat the oven to 325°F.

2. In a small bowl, whisk the peanut butter and 1½ cups of the water until fully combined. Set the peanut sauce aside.

3. In a large Dutch oven or other ovenproof pot, heat the peanut oil over medium-high heat. Once hot, add the steak and sear for a minute on each side, working in batches so as not to crowd the pan. Once seared, transfer the steak to a plate or cutting board and set aside.

4. Add the onion and bell peppers to the pot and sauté for 5 minutes, or until softened. Add the garlic and stir for 1 minute.

5. Add the peanut sauce, salt, hot sauce, and tomatoes and their juices to the pot. Return the steak to the pot and toss gently to coat.

6. Cover the pot, transfer to the oven, and bake for 45 minutes.

7. Remove the pot from the oven and return it to the stove over low heat. Remove the lid and add the potatoes and parsnips. Cook for 30 minutes more, or until the vegetables are fork-tender.

8. Add the spinach, cover the pot, and cook for 5 minutes, or until the spinach wilts. Stir to incorporate.

9. Serve immediately. Store leftovers in an airtight container in the refrigerator for up to 2 days, or in the freezer for up to 1 month.

MAKE-AHEAD TIP: If you're making this dish ahead of time, boil the parsnips and potatoes in advance. Then add them to the dish when you take it out of the oven and skip directly to adding the spinach.

Lamb Tagine

SERVES 4 TO 6 • PREP TIME: 15 MINUTES / COOK TIME: 3 HOURS

When you hear the word "tagine," you might picture the cone-shaped clay pots often used in Moroccan cooking. More broadly, though, tagine refers to the dish cooked inside the pot, usually made with meat, fruit, and vegetables. Here I use a fairly traditional pairing of chickpeas and apricots (prunes or figs work, too). This slow-cooked one-pot dish produces incredibly tender meat and can go straight from the stove to the table. It's low-maintenance but festive—perfect for a holiday meal. Try serving the lamb on top of rice or couscous.

2 tablespoons olive oil

6 lamb shanks

1 onion, coarsely chopped

6 garlic cloves, minced

1 tablespoon finely chopped fresh ginger

1 cinnamon stick

5 teaspoons Chinese five-spice powder

1 (14.5-ounce) can diced tomatoes, undrained

3 cups chicken broth

½ cup dried apricots

1 (15-ounce) can chickpeas, drained and rinsed

1. In a Dutch oven or other large pot, heat the olive oil over medium heat. Once hot, add the lamb shanks and sear for 4 minutes on each side. Remove the lamb from the pot and set aside on a plate or cutting board.

2. Add the onion to the pot and sauté for 5 minutes to soften, using a wooden spoon to release any stuck bits from the bottom of the pot.

3. Add the garlic, ginger, cinnamon stick, and five-spice powder and stir to incorporate. Add the diced tomatoes and their juices, the broth, and the apricots. Return the lamb shanks to the pot and bring to a boil. Once boiling, cover the pot, reduce the heat to low, and simmer for 3 hours (the lamb should reach an internal temperature of 145°F).

4. Remove the stew from the heat and stir in the chickpeas, allowing them to warm through for 2 to 3 minutes.

5. Serve hot. Store leftovers in an airtight container in the refrigerator for 2 to 3 days, or in the freezer for up to 1 month.

COOKING TIP: To speed up the process a bit, you can use cubed lamb stew meat. Sear as directed in step 1. Then, after adding the lamb back to the pot, simmer for only 1½ hours instead of 3 hours.

Melt-in-Your-Mouth Ribs

GLUTEN-FREE, GREAT FOR SHABBAT, WEEKEND

SERVES 6 • PREP TIME: 10 MINUTES / COOK TIME: 3 HOURS

This might be the easiest main-dish recipe in this entire book, and if you have meat lovers in your house, I guarantee it'll become a staple. I was given a version of this recipe from my friend Judith years ago and adjusted it to make it gluten-free for my daughter. Judith's original recipe uses stir-fry sauce in place of one of the jars of barbecue sauce, and her version is amazing, too. I recommend a thick barbecue sauce—my favorite brand is Bone Suckin' Sauce, but you should use your favorite!

2 (16-ounce) jars gluten-free barbecue sauce of your choice

1 (12-ounce) jar tomato-based chili sauce, such as Heinz

5 pounds bone-in beef short ribs

1. Preheat the oven to 300°F.

2. Pour all three bottles of sauce into a large roasting pan and stir to combine. Place the short ribs directly on top of the sauce and spoon some of the sauce over each rib.

3. Cover the roasting pan with aluminum foil, place in the oven, and roast for 3 hours.

4. Serve the ribs immediately, with the sauce from the pan spooned over the top. Store leftovers in an airtight container in the refrigerator for up to 3 days, or freeze in the sauce for up to 4 months.

Sheet Pan Chicken with Root Vegetables and Cabbage

GLUTEN-FREE, WEEKNIGHT

SERVES 4 TO 6 • PREP TIME: 15 MINUTES / COOK TIME: 1 HOUR

Sheet pan meals are some of my favorites for weeknights since I can cook an entire dinner in one pan. This recipe came together as a happy accident on a busy weeknight, when I was trying to use up vegetables left over from a trip to the farmers' market. Try serving with a simple green salad dressed with Perfect Vinaigrette (page 120).

3 pounds thin-sliced chicken breast cutlets

1 head cabbage, thinly sliced

4 carrots, sliced

2 kohlrabi, peeled and cubed

2 teaspoons adobo seasoning

1½ teaspoons freshly ground black pepper

1 teaspoon onion powder

1 teaspoon garlic powder

½ teaspoon sea salt

Olive oil cooking spray

1. Preheat the oven to 375°F. Line a large baking sheet with parchment paper.

2. Arrange the chicken, cabbage, carrots, and kohlrabi on the prepared baking sheet in an even layer.

3. In a small bowl, combine the adobo seasoning, pepper, onion powder, garlic powder, and salt.

4. Lightly mist the chicken and vegetables with cooking spray and sprinkle the seasoning mixture on top.

5. Roast for 1 hour, or until the vegetables are fork-tender and browned and the chicken is cooked through.

6. Serve immediately. Store leftovers in an airtight container in the refrigerator for 1 to 2 days.

VARIATION TIP: Since this dish cooks for an hour, when substituting vegetables, you'll want to choose sturdier varieties that can withstand a long cooking time. Broccoli, squash, beets, and sweet potatoes are all great choices.

Mom's Fried Chicken
with Lemon Sauce

GREAT FOR SHABBAT, WEEKEND

SERVES 6 • PREP TIME: 30 MINUTES / COOK TIME: 1 HOUR

My mother serves this chicken on every holiday, and no matter how much she makes, there's never any left over. It's like an upgraded take on schnitzel. This recipe is for six cutlets, but I often double or triple it, because we usually want more (leftovers freeze well, so don't worry about making too much). This dish is quite simple to put together and remains one of my family's favorites.

6 thin-sliced chicken breast cutlets

2 large eggs

2 cups matzoh meal

1 teaspoon sea salt

1 teaspoon garlic powder

½ teaspoon dried oregano

½ teaspoon dried parsley

½ teaspoon freshly ground black pepper

¼ cup avocado oil

Juice of 1 large lemon

¾ cup chicken broth

½ cup white wine

1. Preheat the oven to 350°F. Line a large baking sheet with parchment paper.

2. If the chicken cutlets are not already thin (they need to be ⅛ inch thick), use a meat pounder or metal bowl to pound them as thin as you can.

3. In a medium bowl, beat the eggs until no visible whites remain.

4. In a separate medium bowl, combine the matzoh meal, salt, garlic powder, oregano, parsley, and pepper and stir to combine.

5. Dip each cutlet into the eggs and then into the matzoh meal mixture, evenly coating both sides. Once coated, place the cutlets on the prepared baking sheet.

6. In a large ovenproof skillet, heat the avocado oil over medium-high heat. Once hot, add the breaded cutlets to the skillet, working in batches to prevent overcrowding. Shallow-fry the chicken for 2 minutes on each side, until just golden brown. Once fried, return the chicken to the baking sheet.

7. Pour any excess oil out of the skillet, but keep the crunchy drippings in the pan. Add the lemon juice, broth, and wine and stir to incorporate. Use a wooden spoon to make sure any stuck-on drippings are incorporated.

8. Return the chicken to the skillet and turn to coat in the sauce. Cover with aluminum foil, transfer to the oven, and bake for 30 minutes.

9. Remove the foil and bake for 15 minutes more.

10. Serve immediately. Store leftovers in an airtight container in the refrigerator for up to 3 days, or in the freezer for up to 2 months.

INGREDIENT TIP: For a gluten-free version, use gluten-free matzoh meal or bread crumbs, available online or at kosher or specialty stores.

Jenny's Chicken Pelau

GLUTEN-FREE, WEEKNIGHT

SERVES 4 • PREP TIME: 15 MINUTES / COOK TIME: 45 MINUTES

Chicken pelau is a Trinidadian dish made with meat, rice, and pigeon peas in a burnt sugar sauce. I got this recipe from my eldest child's baby nurse, Jenny, who made a version for us using all-kosher ingredients. The results were absolutely delicious—my husband said it was one of the best dinners he had ever had. This version of the dish is taken from the notes I scribbled down while I watched Jenny cook, and I still make it to this day.

2 tablespoons avocado oil

1 onion, coarsely chopped

2 tablespoons light brown sugar

1½ pounds boneless, skinless chicken thighs

4 scallions, chopped

2 celery stalks, chopped

3 garlic cloves, minced

1 (15-ounce) can pigeon peas, drained and rinsed

1 (13-ounce) can full-fat coconut milk

2 cups rice

1 (8.75-ounce) can corn kernels, drained

1 teaspoon sea salt

1 teaspoon dried thyme

1. In a large pot, heat the avocado oil over medium heat. Once hot, add the onion and sauté for 5 minutes, or until softened.

2. Add the brown sugar and stir it until it liquefies and starts to caramelize. Add the chicken thighs and stir to coat them in the sugar. Add the scallions, celery, garlic, pigeon peas, and coconut milk and stir to incorporate. Cook for 10 minutes, stirring occasionally.

3. Add the rice, corn, salt, thyme, and enough water to just reach the top of the ingredients. Bring the mixture to a boil. Once boiling, reduce the heat to low, cover, and simmer for about 30 minutes, until the rice and chicken are cooked through.

4. Serve the chicken pelau hot. Store leftovers in an airtight container in the refrigerator for up to 3 days.

VARIATION TIP: You can make pelau with any other meat, like beef stew meat or chicken legs.

Honey-Mustard Chicken with Shiitake Mushrooms

GLUTEN-FREE, WEEKNIGHT

SERVES 4 • PREP TIME: 15 MINUTES / COOK TIME: 45 MINUTES

This one-pan recipe is quick and easy to make and is a crowd-pleaser for adults and kids alike. It's worth investing in a brand of honey mustard you really like— my personal favorite is the brand Honeycup. It's thick and sweet-but-not-too-sweet, and provides the tanginess this dish needs. I like to serve this chicken over egg noodles, which are great for absorbing the sauce.

1 teaspoon paprika

½ teaspoon parsley flakes

½ teaspoon garlic powder

½ teaspoon freshly ground black pepper

¼ teaspoon sea salt

6 thin-sliced chicken breast cutlets (about 5 ounces each)

2 tablespoons olive oil

1 (8-ounce) package shiitake mush-rooms, sliced

6 scallions, chopped

2 tablespoons honey mustard

¼ cup white wine

1½ cups chicken broth

1. In a small bowl, combine the paprika, parsley flakes, garlic powder, pepper, and salt and mix to incorporate. Dredge the chicken cutlets in the spice mixture to coat evenly on both sides.

2. In a large skillet, heat the olive oil over medium heat. Once hot, add the chicken cutlets to the skillet. Cook the chicken for about 3 minutes on each side, just to brown the outside. Remove the chicken from the skillet and set aside.

3. Add the mushrooms to the skillet and sauté for 3 minutes, or until softened. Add the scallions and stir to incorporate. Add the honey mustard and the wine and stir to coat.

4. Return the chicken to the skillet and pour in the broth. Bring the mixture to a boil, then reduce the heat to maintain a simmer, cover, and cook for 20 minutes, or until the chicken is cooked through.

5. Serve hot. Store leftovers in an airtight container in the refrigerator for 2 to 3 days.

INGREDIENT TIP: If you do not have honey mustard, you can make your own: Mix 2 parts mustard to 1 part honey.

Braised Cornish Hens with Dates and Cherries

GLUTEN-FREE, GREAT FOR SHABBAT, WEEKEND

SERVES 4 • PREP TIME: 15 MINUTES / COOK TIME: 1 HOUR 30 MINUTES

This festive recipe is one of my favorites for Rosh Hashanah, since the sweet dates and cherries symbolize a sweet new year. The dish looks stunning on a plate, and it has an incredible flavor to match. This recipe also works great for Sukkot because of the fruits, but I also sometimes make a dressed-down version for Shabbat dinner, using mixed bone-in chicken pieces instead of Cornish hens (you can do the same if you can't find Cornish hens).

4 Cornish hens

½ teaspoon sea salt

½ teaspoon freshly ground black pepper

½ cup dried cherries

½ cup pitted dates

¼ cup orange juice

Juice of 2 limes

1½ cups chicken broth

½ cup white wine

1. Preheat the oven to 375°F.

2. Set the Cornish hens in a large roasting pan and season them with the salt and pepper. Roast for 30 minutes.

3. Meanwhile, in a medium saucepan, combine the cherries, dates, orange juice, lime juice, broth, and wine. Cook, stirring occasionally, for 15 minutes, until the dates start to break down and the sauce thickens.

4. Remove the roasting pan from the oven and pour the sauce over the Cornish hens. Return them to the oven and roast for 1 hour more. Every 20 minutes, baste them with the sauce. Once finished, the internal temperature of the thighs should read 165°F.

5. Serve hot. Store leftovers in an airtight container in the refrigerator for 2 days, or in the freezer for up to 1 month.

VARIATION TIP: If you do not have an aversion to prunes, they work really well as a substitute for dates in this recipe. The cooking caramelizes them nicely.

Oven-Roasted Chicken with Mushrooms and Tomatoes

GLUTEN-FREE, WEEKNIGHT

SERVES 4 TO 6 • PREP TIME: 15 MINUTES / COOK TIME: 45 MINUTES

This is one of my favorite easy dinners, and I make some variation of it at least once a week. It's hands-off—most of the work is done in the oven—and it relies on pantry staples, so I never have to worry about a last-minute trip to the grocery store. Feel free to substitute almost any vegetable you have on hand, like bell peppers, artichoke hearts, or zucchini. Try serving this dish with Mustard-Spiced Roasted Potatoes (page 40).

1 (8-ounce) package cremini mushrooms, sliced, or 2 (4-ounce) cans sliced mushrooms

2 red onions, thinly sliced

6 boneless, skinless chicken thighs (6 to 8 ounces each)

½ teaspoon sea salt

½ teaspoon freshly ground black pepper

1 tablespoon finely chopped fresh basil, or 1 teaspoon dried

¼ cup olive oil

6 plum tomatoes, sliced

1 teaspoon dried oregano

1. Preheat the oven to 375°F.

2. In a roasting pan or 9-by-13-inch baking dish, combine the mushrooms and onions. Place the chicken thighs on top and season with the salt and pepper. Sprinkle with the basil. Drizzle the olive oil over the chicken. Top with the tomatoes and sprinkle with the oregano.

3. Cover the roasting pan or dish with aluminum foil and roast for 30 minutes.

4. Uncover and roast for an additional 15 to 20 minutes, or until the internal temperature of the chicken reaches 165°F.

5. Serve hot. Store leftovers in an airtight container in the refrigerator for up to 2 days.

COOKING TIP: I recommend a glass baking dish (such as Pyrex) for this recipe—the sauce from the vegetables that collects at the bottom doesn't seem to stick to glass as much, making cleanup easier.

Chicken and Cilantro Rice

GLUTEN-FREE, GREAT FOR SHABBAT,
WEEKEND, WEEKNIGHT

SERVES 4 TO 6 • PREP TIME: 10 MINUTES / COOK TIME: 3 HOURS

This is my kids' and my husband's favorite meal—they request it almost every Friday. The cooking time is on the longer side, but the process itself is hands-off, and the chicken comes out so tender that it's well worth the wait. The rice is key for flavor here, as it absorbs all the fat from the chicken, which adds extra richness to this crowd-pleasing dish.

2 pounds bone-in, skin-on chicken parts, such as drumsticks, thighs, and breasts

2 onions, coarsely chopped

Leaves from 1 bunch cilantro, coarsely chopped

6 garlic cloves, minced

2 cups brown rice

½ cup avocado oil

1 tablespoon ground turmeric

1 teaspoon sea salt

1 teaspoon freshly ground black pepper

3 cups water

1. Preheat the oven to 350°F.

2. Place the chicken in a large roasting pan or Dutch oven. Add the onions, cilantro, garlic, rice, avocado oil, turmeric, salt, and pepper. Add the water and cover the pan with aluminum foil or a lid.

3. Transfer the pan to the oven and bake for 1 hour 30 minutes.

4. Remove from the oven, uncover, and stir to mix everything together. Cover, return to the oven, and bake for 1 hour 30 minutes more—the internal temperature of the chicken should reach 165°F.

5. Serve hot. Store leftovers in an airtight container in the refrigerator for 2 to 3 days.

COOKING TIP: I don't suggest freezing this dish, as the texture of the rice will change. If you don't want to cut up the chicken beforehand, you can also roughly cut it directly in the dish after it comes out of the oven.

Cinnamon Crumb Challah 102

CHAPTER 7

Breads, Pastries, and Desserts

I could've included enough recipes in this chapter to take up this entire cookbook, which means the ten that made it in are the very best of the best. I deliberately chose versatile recipes that are easily adapted to fit different ingredients or taste preferences. Take the Cinnamon Crumb Challah, for example: The recipe is for a challah with a sugary crumb topping, but it also makes an excellent base for a savory challah as well. The title of the Almost-Any-Fruit Crumble speaks for itself: It's designed to showcase whatever seasonal fruit you have available. Even the vegan Chai Chocolate Mousse can be adapted using your favorite kind of tea to change up the flavor. Finally, I know that many nonkosher cookbooks use dairy heavily in pastries and desserts, so I made sure that all ten recipes are pareve, making them perfect to enjoy with any meal.

Cinnamon Crumb Challah

GREAT FOR SHABBAT, PAREVE, VEGETARIAN

MAKES 4 MEDIUM LOAVES • PREP TIME: 30 MINUTES,
PLUS 3 HOURS TO RISE / COOK TIME: 40 MINUTES

This challah will make your house smell like a bakery. If you've never baked your own challah before, don't be intimidated—the process is time-consuming (you'll need 4 to 5 hours), but the steps themselves are simple. The base recipe without the topping works great for savory challah—bake it plain or sprinkle with everything bagel seasoning. Save leftovers for Overnight Apple Challah French Toast (page 23). Note: This recipe doesn't make enough for the weekly blessing on the challah (called "taking challah"), which ancient tradition dictates must be made with a whole bag of flour (more than 14 cups in modern times). In order to get to the required amount of flour, you will need to double this recipe.

For the challah dough

3 (7-gram) envelopes active dry yeast (about 2¼ tablespoons)

1½ cups warm water

¾ cup honey, divided

½ cup vegetable oil, plus more for greasing the bowl

4 large eggs

1 cup unflavored seltzer

1 teaspoon sea salt

10 cups all-purpose flour

For the cinnamon crumb topping

½ cup coconut oil, at room temperature

1 teaspoon vanilla extract

2 tablespoons ground cinnamon

1 cup sugar

1¼ cups all-purpose flour

Egg wash: 1 large egg yolk beaten with 1 tablespoon water

1. **To make the challah dough:** In a large bowl, mix the yeast, warm water, and ¼ cup of the honey. Let it rest for 5 minutes.

2. Add the remaining ½ cup honey, the oil, eggs, seltzer, salt, and 2 cups of the flour to the bowl. Mix to combine. Continue adding the flour 2 cups at a time, mixing after each addition, until a soft dough is formed. Knead with your hands until the dough comes together—it should be smooth and less sticky. Depending on your kneading, this can take 10 to 15 minutes. (You can also knead using a stand mixer fitted with the dough hook for 8 to 10 minutes.)

3. Clean out the bowl and grease it with oil. Return the dough to the bowl and cover it with parchment paper or a clean kitchen towel. Let the dough rise until doubled in size, about 1 hour 30 minutes.

4. **To make the cinnamon crumb topping:** In a medium bowl, stir together the coconut oil, vanilla, cinnamon, sugar, and flour. Mix until thoroughly combined and set aside.

5. **To form the loaves:** Line two 18-by-13-inch baking sheets with parchment paper.

6. Once the dough has risen, divide it into 4 equal portions—one for each loaf. Divide each portion into thirds for braiding (you will have 12 portions altogether). Roll each portion between your hands to form a long rope.

7. To braid the loaves, take 3 ropes and pinch them together at one end. Braid like you would braid hair—take the right strand and bring it over the middle strand so it becomes the middle strand. Do the same with the left strand, so it becomes the middle strand. Repeat until you get to the end of the ropes; then pinch the strands together at the end. Repeat with the remaining ropes to make three more challahs.

8. Place two challahs on each of the prepared baking sheets. Brush the tops of the challahs with the egg wash and top with the cinnamon crumb topping. Cover the braided challahs with parchment or clean kitchen towels and allow them to rise until doubled in size, about 1 hour 30 minutes.

9. When the challahs are almost finished rising, preheat the oven to 350°F.

10. Bake for 30 to 40 minutes, until the challahs are golden brown and feel hollow when knocked. Serve warm or at room temperature. Store extra challah in airtight zip-top bags in the freezer for up to 2 months.

VARIATION TIP: If you don't want to braid the challahs, you can purchase a challah mold, available online and at most kosher stores. Alternatively, use round metal cake pans to make pull-apart challahs: Grease 4 to 6 cake pans with oil (6-, 8-, and 10-inch sizes all work). Roll pieces of the challah dough into 2-inch balls and place them in the prepared pans. Bake at 350°F for 25 to 40 minutes (depending on the size of the pans), until golden brown.

Herbed Focaccia

PAREVE, VEGETARIAN, WEEKEND, WEEKNIGHT

SERVES 4 TO 6 • PREP TIME: 15 MINUTES, PLUS 1 HOUR
30 MINUTES TO RISE / COOK TIME: 55 MINUTES

Focaccia is one of the easiest breads to make, so if you're a beginner, this is a great place to start. I use olives and tomatoes here, but you can top your focaccia with almost anything, like onions, eggplant, or herbs and spices. This recipe is the perfect accompaniment to soup or any of the spreads in chapter 8, such as Garlicky Eggplant Spread (page 118), Red Pepper Spread (page 119), or 3-Ingredient Olive Dip (page 121).

1 (7-gram) envelope active dry yeast
   (about 2¼ teaspoons)
1½ cups warm water
3½ cups all-purpose flour
2 teaspoons sea salt

4 tablespoons olive oil, divided, plus more
   for the pan
1 (3.8-ounce) can sliced pitted olives
3 plum tomatoes, sliced

1. In a large bowl, stir together the yeast and warm water. Let sit for 5 minutes to rehydrate the yeast.

2. Add the flour, salt, and 1 tablespoon of the olive oil and mix until fully incorporated, then begin kneading by hand directly in the bowl. Once the dough forms a solid mass, cover the bowl with a piece of parchment paper or a clean kitchen towel. Let the dough rise for 30 minutes.

3. Knead the dough in the bowl for a few minutes, then cover and let it rise for another 30 minutes (it won't double in size, just puff up).

4. Meanwhile, preheat the oven to 375°F. Grease an 18-by-13-inch baking sheet with olive oil.

5. Use your hands to scoop the dough onto the prepared pan and spread it into an even layer. Using your fingertips, poke the dough to make dimples all over its surface. Drizzle the remaining 3 tablespoons olive oil over the dough. Let rise for 20 minutes.

6. Top the focaccia with the olives and tomatoes. Bake for 10 minutes. Reduce the oven temperature to 350°F and bake for 45 minutes more, or until the top is golden brown.

7. Cut the focaccia into squares or strips. Serve hot. Wrap leftovers airtight and store in the refrigerator for up to 5 days, or in the freezer for up to 2 months.

MAKE-AHEAD TIP: This is a great recipe to bake in multiple batches, using different toppings for each. Cut them in squares, freeze them, and thaw just in time for a meal!

Chocolate Chip Mandelbread Squares

GREAT FOR SHABBAT, PAREVE, VEGETARIAN, WEEKEND, WEEKNIGHT

MAKES 24 COOKIES • PREP TIME: 10 MINUTES / COOK TIME: 40 MINUTES

These little mandelbread squares are the perfect dessert for when you need a quick bite to satisfy your sweet tooth. I've been making these cookies for years, and they're still among my favorites, with crispy golden brown edges and a soft center. I keep a batch ready in the freezer in case guests stop by unexpectedly or my kids bring friends over after school. Be warned that making these will cause your entire house to smell like cookies.

1 cup sugar

1 cup grapeseed oil

3 large eggs

3 cups all-purpose flour

1 teaspoon baking powder

1½ teaspoons vanilla extract

1 (10-ounce) package pareve chocolate chips

1. Preheat the oven to 325°F. Line an 18-by-13-inch baking sheet with parchment paper.

2. In a large bowl, mix together the sugar, grapeseed oil, eggs, flour, baking powder, vanilla, and chocolate chips until all the ingredients are fully incorporated. A somewhat thick dough will form.

3. Spread the dough into the prepared pan, pressing it into an even layer—it should be between ⅛ and ¼ inch thick, depending on your preference. Bake for 30 minutes.

4. Remove the mandelbread from the oven (it should only be partially baked) and leave the oven on. Cut the mandelbread into 24 squares and return the pan to the oven to bake for another 5 minutes, or until just golden around the edges.

5. Enjoy immediately or let cool for about 15 minutes and enjoy at room temperature. Store leftovers in an airtight container at room temperature for a few days, or in the freezer for up to 3 months.

VARIATION TIP: For gluten-free mandelbread (and to make these kosher for Passover), replace the flour with the same amount of almond flour or another grain-free flour—my favorite brand is Rorie's, available online or in most kosher stores.

Chai Chocolate Mousse

GLUTEN-FREE, GREAT FOR SHABBAT, PAREVE, VEGETARIAN,
WEEKEND, WEEKNIGHT

SERVES 4 • PREP TIME: 30 MINUTES, PLUS 2 HOURS TO SET

It's nearly impossible to find a pareve dessert that is easy, delicious, and healthy. That's why this mousse is special—it somehow meets all three criteria. The secret here is aquafaba, the liquid from a can of chickpeas (so don't throw that liquid away!). When beaten, aquafaba takes on a frothy, whipped consistency that can be used as a vegan substitute for egg whites or whipped cream in desserts. When I have company, I like to serve the mousse in martini glasses topped with berries.

1 cup aquafaba (liquid from two 15-ounce cans chickpeas)

4 chai tea bags

1 tablespoon coconut oil

1 (9-ounce) package pareve bittersweet or dark chocolate chips

1. In a small pot, combine the aquafaba and the tea bags. Simmer over medium-low heat for 5 minutes to allow the tea to steep.

2. In a microwave-safe bowl, combine the coconut oil and the chocolate chips. Microwave in 30-second intervals, stirring after each, until fully melted and combined (it should take 2 to 3 minutes total).

3. Remove the aquafaba mixture from the heat and discard the tea bags. Transfer the mixture to a stand mixer (or to a medium bowl and use a hand mixer), and whip the aquafaba until it doubles in volume—it should be foamy and form peaks.

4. Gently fold the melted chocolate into the whipped aquafaba until incorporated, being careful not to overmix. Spoon the mousse into four ramekins and refrigerate for at least 2 hours to set before serving. The mousse will keep, covered, in the refrigerator for up to 3 days.

VARIATION TIP: You can use any type of tea to flavor the aquafaba—just be sure to choose something that will complement the mousse's chocolate flavor.

Almost-Any-Fruit Crumble

GREAT FOR SHABBAT, PAREVE, VEGETARIAN,
WEEKEND, WEEKNIGHT

SERVES 4 TO 6 • PREP TIME: 15 MINUTES / COOK TIME: 30 MINUTES

I love fruit crumbles because they're versatile by design. I recommend using whatever fruit is in season: In the summer, I use berries, peaches, and nectarines; in the fall, apples, and in the winter, pears. I often make a larger batch of the crumb topping to freeze (it will keep for up to 3 months) so I can throw a crumble in the oven anytime. The crumb topping is also delicious over fruit or layered in trifle—it may become a staple of your freezer, too.

For the filling

Coconut oil, for the baking dish

6 cups diced fruit of your choice

¼ cup sugar

1 tablespoon all-purpose flour

Grated zest and juice of 1 lemon

For the crumb topping

1¼ cups all-purpose flour

1 cup sugar

2 tablespoons ground cinnamon

½ cup coconut oil, at room temperature

1 teaspoon vanilla extract

1. Preheat the oven to 375°F. Lightly grease a 9-inch square baking dish with coconut oil.

2. **To make the filling:** In a large bowl, toss the fruit with the sugar, flour, lemon zest, and lemon juice.

3. **To make the crumb topping:** In a medium bowl, mix together the flour, sugar, cinnamon, coconut oil, and vanilla until fully incorporated. Set aside.

4. Transfer the filling to the baking dish and spread it into an even layer. Sprinkle the crumb topping evenly over the fruit.

5. Bake the crumble for about 30 minutes, until the fruit is bubbling and the topping is browned. Serve hot. Store leftovers in an airtight container in the refrigerator for up to 3 days.

Grandma Dotty's Brownies

GREAT FOR SHABBAT, PAREVE, VEGETARIAN,
WEEKEND, WEEKNIGHT

MAKES 12 BROWNIES • PREP TIME: 20 MINUTES, PLUS 15 MINUTES
TO COOL / COOK TIME: 30 MINUTES

I have the fondest memories of these brownies. Whenever I went to my grandmother's house as a kid, she always had brownies in the freezer as a treat. Her original recipe called for margarine, but I've omitted that here to make it a little healthier (I am a nutritionist, after all). I dare say this updated version is just as delicious as Grandma Dotty's and, like hers, keeps very well in the freezer. Feel free to use nuts instead of chocolate chips.

1 cup coconut oil, plus more for the pan

1 cup all-purpose flour, plus more for the pan

4 ounces pareve bittersweet chocolate, roughly broken into 1-inch pieces

4 large eggs

1½ cups sugar

1½ teaspoons vanilla extract

1 cup pareve chocolate chips

1. Preheat the oven to 350°F. Grease a 9-inch square baking pan with coconut oil and dust with flour, tapping out any excess.

2. In a small pot, combine the bittersweet chocolate and coconut oil. Heat over medium-low heat, stirring occasionally, until fully melted and combined, about 5 minutes. Remove from the heat and set aside.

3. In a large bowl, whisk together the eggs and sugar until fully incorporated. Add the melted chocolate mixture and whisk to incorporate. Stir in the vanilla.

4. Add the flour in batches to ensure even mixing, stirring until fully incorporated after each addition. Stir in the chocolate chips.

5. Pour the batter into the prepared baking pan and bake for 30 minutes. Let cool for 15 minutes before cutting into 12 squares. Serve warm, at room temperature, or chilled. Store leftovers in an airtight container in the refrigerator for up to 4 days, or in the freezer for up to 3 months.

VARIATION TIP: Make these brownies gluten-free by subbing out the flour for a 1:1 gluten-free flour. You can even bake these with almond flour to make them kosher for Passover.

Peanut Butter Cookies

GLUTEN-FREE, GREAT FOR SHABBAT, PAREVE,
VEGETARIAN, WEEKEND, WEEKNIGHT

MAKES ABOUT 12 COOKIES • PREP TIME: 15 MINUTES / COOK TIME: 12 TO 15 MINUTES

Finding a good gluten-free cookie recipe that doesn't involve a million different kinds of flour can be challenging, but your search is over—the recipe is right here. These cookies are so easy to make (and so delicious!) that my kids have been known to whip up a batch or two themselves. This is a super-quick recipe to make last-minute whenever a craving hits.

2 cups peanut butter

1½ cups sugar

2 large eggs

1 teaspoon baking soda

½ teaspoon sea salt

½ cup gluten-free rolled oats

1½ cups pareve chocolate chips

1 cup peanuts

1. Preheat the oven to 350°F. Line a baking sheet with parchment paper.

2. In a large bowl, combine the peanut butter, sugar, eggs, baking soda, salt, and oats. Use a wooden spoon or spatula to stir until the mixture is thoroughly incorporated—the dough should be thick. Stir in the chocolate chips and peanuts.

3. Using a tablespoon, scoop out mounds of the cookie dough and place them on the prepared baking sheet, spacing them 1 inch apart. You should have about 12 cookies.

4. Bake the cookies for 12 to 15 minutes, until they're just golden on the edges. Serve warm. Store leftovers in an airtight container in the refrigerator for up to 4 days, or in the freezer for up to 3 months.

VARIATION TIP: If you have a peanut allergy, not to worry—you can sub in any nut or seed butter; replace the peanuts with the corresponding nut butter or seed.

Peach Torte

GREAT FOR SHABBAT, PAREVE, VEGETARIAN,
WEEKEND, WEEKNIGHT

SERVES 6 TO 8 • PREP TIME: 15 MINUTES, PLUS 30 MINUTES
TO COOL / COOK TIME: 45 MINUTES

Everyone should make this cake—it's especially great during the summer, when peaches are at peak season (though you can also use nectarines). If you don't have fresh peaches, a 15-ounce can of peaches works nearly as well. You can make this torte in any round pan, but a springform pan lined with parchment paper is easiest for serving and storing, because you can slide the parchment right off the pan base. Whichever pan you use, be sure to line it and grease it generously to prevent sticking.

2 tablespoons avocado oil

½ cup coconut oil

1 cup sugar, plus 1 tablespoon

1 cup all-purpose flour

2 large eggs

1 teaspoon baking powder

4 peaches, peeled, pitted, and halved or sliced into wedges

Grated zest of 1 lemon

1. Preheat the oven to 350°F. Line the bottom of a 9-inch springform pan with parchment paper. To do this, open the springform ring and place a piece of parchment over the base; then reattach the ring. Trim the excess paper from around the edges. Generously grease the parchment and the sides of the pan with the avocado oil.

2. In a large bowl, combine the coconut oil, 1 cup of the sugar, the flour, eggs, and baking powder. Mix until all the ingredients are fully incorporated.

3. Pour the batter into the prepared pan and spread it into an even layer. Place the peaches on top of the batter (if using wedges, arrange them in concentric circles). Sprinkle the top with the remaining 1 tablespoon sugar and the lemon zest.

4. Bake the torte for 45 minutes, or until the top is golden and a toothpick inserted into the center comes out clean. Cool the cake in the pan on a wire rack for at least 30 minutes before removing the springform ring.

5. Serve at room temperature, or even chilled. The torte will keep in the refrigerator for up to 3 days, or wrap it tightly in a layer of plastic wrap followed by a layer of aluminum foil, then freeze for up to 1 month.

Pareve Ice Cream Pie

GREAT FOR SHABBAT, PAREVE, VEGETARIAN,
WEEKEND, WEEKNIGHT

SERVES 4 TO 6 • PREP TIME: 15 MINUTES, PLUS 3 HOURS TO FREEZE

This might be the easiest dessert of all time—it's low effort but a real showstopper, so I make it whenever my daughters or I have friends visiting. Good pareve desserts can feel hard to come by, but this is without a doubt one of the most delicious ones out there. Any nondairy ice cream will work, but I personally use the brand So Delicious because they have so many flavors. Try using two different flavors together to see which combinations you like!

2 pints nondairy ice cream

1 cup nut butter of your choice

¼ cup powdered sugar

1½ cups pareve chocolate chips

1 (9-inch) store-bought graham
  cracker crust

1. In a stand mixer (or in a large bowl using a hand mixer), mix together the ice cream, nut butter, powdered sugar, and chocolate chips on medium-low speed until all the ingredients are fully incorporated.

2. Using a rubber spatula, transfer the mixture to the graham cracker crust and spread in an even layer. Freeze until set, about 3 hours, before slicing and serving.

VARIATION TIP: Try switching out the graham cracker crust for a chocolate cookie crust (such as Oreo).

Tahini Chocolate Chip Blondies

GREAT FOR SHABBAT, PAREVE, VEGETARIAN,
WEEKEND, WEEKNIGHT

MAKES 12 BLONDIES • PREP TIME: 20 MINUTES, PLUS 15 MINUTES
TO COOL / COOK TIME: 30 MINUTES

These blondies are a perfect combination of two of my other favorite desserts: They taste like chocolate chip cookies, but they have the fudgy consistency of brownies. This is a great dessert for people who like a subtle savory element to complement their desserts—the earthy, nutty taste of the tahini cuts through the sweetness.

½ cup grapeseed oil, plus more for the pan

½ cup applesauce

¾ cup granulated sugar

¾ cup packed light brown sugar

2 teaspoons vanilla extract

2 large eggs

5 tablespoons tahini

2¼ cups all-purpose flour

1 teaspoon baking soda

1 teaspoon sea salt

2 cups pareve chocolate chips

1. Preheat the oven to 375°F. Grease a 9-by-13-inch baking pan with grapeseed oil.

2. In a large bowl using a hand mixer, beat together the grapeseed oil, applesauce, granulated sugar, brown sugar, vanilla, and eggs until the mixture is light and fluffy, 2 to 3 minutes. Beat in the tahini until fully incorporated.

3. Working in batches, add the flour, baking soda, and salt to the bowl. Stir to incorporate until a batter forms. Stir in the chocolate chips.

4. Pour the batter into the prepared baking pan and spread it into an even layer. Bake for about 30 minutes, until golden brown on top and a toothpick inserted into the center comes out clean.

5. Allow the blondies to cool for 15 minutes before cutting into 12 squares. Serve warm or at room temperature. Store leftovers in an airtight container at room temperature for up to 5 days, or in the freezer for up to 2 months.

Red Pepper Spread 119

CHAPTER 8

Sauces, Dips, and Dressings

The dips, sauces, and spreads in this chapter are true staples, integral to my everyday cooking. There are several that I've made for countless Shabbats, including the Garlicky Eggplant Spread, Red Pepper Spread, and 3-Ingredient Olive Dip. I hope these staples will become a part of your everyday cooking repertoire, too. I've included suggestions for how to use these staples in recipe headnotes throughout the book, but I encourage you to get creative, adding them to your own dishes or adjusting the ingredients to suit your taste. For instance, try using the Perfect Vinaigrette as a marinade for chicken, or use the Barbecue Ranch Sauce as a dip for latkes. Most of the recipes make fairly large batches (between 1 and 4 cups), so you'll have plenty of extras for experimentation.

Barbecue Ranch Sauce

GREAT FOR SHABBAT, PAREVE, WEEKEND, WEEKNIGHT

MAKES 1½ CUPS • PREP TIME: 15 MINUTES, PLUS 30 MINUTES
TO COOL / COOK TIME: 30 MINUTES

I have to admit that this sauce was developed by accident. I'd made both barbecue sauce and pareve ranch dressing for a summer barbecue. My youngest daughter put some of each on her plate and mixed them together to dip her chicken in, inadvertently creating my next recipe. It was so tasty that when I was cleaning up, I mixed the leftovers together. It's now a staple in our house—try with Vegetarian "Crab" Cakes (page 75) or Rice Bowls with Avocado Dressing (page 78).

¼ cup avocado oil

1 medium onion, finely diced

¼ cup apple cider vinegar

Juice of ½ lemon

Juice of 1 lime

½ cup water

1 tablespoon Dijon mustard

1½ teaspoons sea salt

1½ teaspoons freshly ground black pepper

1 teaspoon chili powder

½ cup tomato-based chili sauce, such as Heinz

1½ teaspoons liquid smoke

2 tablespoons Pareve Worcestershire sauce

½ cup mayonnaise

1. In a medium pot, warm the avocado oil over medium heat. Once hot, add the onion and sauté for 5 minutes, or until softened.

2. Add the vinegar, lemon juice, lime juice, water, mustard, salt, pepper, and chili powder. Bring the mixture to a boil, then reduce the heat to low and simmer for 20 minutes. The mixture will reduce and begin to thicken.

3. Stir in the chili sauce, liquid smoke, and Worcestershire sauce. Return to a boil, then immediately remove from the heat and set aside to cool for 30 minutes.

4. Once the mixture is cool, whisk in the mayonnaise until thoroughly incorporated. Transfer to a jar and store in the refrigerator for up to 1 week.

Not-Your-Ordinary Pesto

GLUTEN-FREE, GREAT FOR SHABBAT, PAREVE, VEGETARIAN,
WEEKEND, WEEKNIGHT

MAKES 2 CUPS • PREP TIME: 10 MINUTES / COOK TIME: 10 MINUTES

I love pesto, but traditional versions usually include Parmesan cheese, which is a no-go for meat meals. I created this vegan version for snacking between meals on a Shabbat afternoon, to eat with veggies or rice cakes. Nutritional yeast provides a cheesy, nutty substitute for Parmesan and is also a terrific source of B vitamins. This version uses parsley, but for a traditional take, you can use the same amount of basil instead—it works just as well.

1 cup walnuts

1 cup fresh parsley or cilantro leaves (or a combination)

4 garlic cloves, peeled

2 tablespoons nutritional yeast

½ cup olive oil

Juice of ½ lemon

1 teaspoon sea salt

½ teaspoon freshly ground black pepper

1. Preheat the oven to 400°F. Line a baking sheet with parchment paper.

2. Spread the walnuts over the prepared baking sheet and toast in the oven just until browned. This usually takes between 5 and 10 minutes, depending on your oven, but keep a close eye on them so you can catch them before they burn.

3. In a food processor, combine the toasted walnuts, parsley, garlic, nutritional yeast, olive oil, lemon juice, salt, and pepper. Pulse until completely smooth. Serve with bread, protein, or veggies. Store in an airtight container in the refrigerator for up to 5 days.

VARIATION TIP: The flavor possibilities are endless for this pesto. Try adding jarred red peppers, sun-dried tomatoes, or pitted olives to the food processor—all are delicious!

Garlicky Eggplant Spread

GLUTEN-FREE, GREAT FOR SHABBAT, PAREVE, VEGETARIAN, WEEKEND, WEEKNIGHT

MAKES 2 CUPS (SERVES 4 TO 6) • PREP TIME: 20 MINUTES / COOK TIME: 1 HOUR

This eggplant spread is an absolute crowd-pleaser every time. Eggplant is a great base for a chunky dip because as it breaks down, it takes on and amplifies whatever flavors you add to it. I often make this spread to serve with challah on Friday nights, but it's also perfect as a dip for pita chips and veggies. My kids have even been known to eat it with plain grilled chicken.

2 eggplants, peeled and cubed

2 sweet onions, cubed

4 garlic cloves, peeled

¼ cup olive oil

1 teaspoon sea salt

½ teaspoon freshly ground black pepper

2 tablespoons tomato paste

1. Preheat the oven to 375°F. Line an 18-by-13-inch baking sheet with parchment paper.

2. In a large bowl, combine the eggplant, onions, garlic, olive oil, salt, and pepper and toss to thoroughly coat.

3. Spread the eggplant and onions in a single layer on the prepared pan. Roast for 1 hour, or until the eggplant has browned and the flesh has started to break down.

4. Transfer the eggplant mixture to a food processor or blender. Add the tomato paste and pulse until fully incorporated and smooth. Serve with bread or vegetables. Store in an airtight container in the refrigerator for up to 4 days.

Red Pepper Spread

GLUTEN-FREE, GREAT FOR SHABBAT, PAREVE, VEGETARIAN, WEEKEND, WEEKNIGHT

MAKES 2 CUPS (SERVES 4 TO 6) • PREP TIME: 5 MINUTES, PLUS 15 MINUTES TO COOL / COOK TIME: 10 MINUTES

During Friday Shabbat dinners, it's common to put a variety of dips and spreads on the table to eat as a first course with salad and challah. My house is no exception! This red pepper spread is one of my favorites—it's great with cut fresh veggies like celery and carrots, on challah, or even as a sandwich spread. I usually make extra to enjoy all week long. If you prefer a creamier spread, add 2 tablespoons mayonnaise when you puree the peppers.

2 tablespoons olive oil

1 green bell pepper, coarsely chopped

2 red bell peppers, coarsely chopped

4 garlic cloves, chopped

1 teaspoon ground cumin

½ teaspoon sea salt

½ teaspoon freshly ground black pepper

1. In a large skillet, combine the oil, bell peppers, and garlic. Sauté over medium heat for 5 minutes, or until the peppers are softened. Set aside for 15 minutes to cool.

2. Once cooled, transfer the bell pepper mixture to a food processor. Add the cumin, salt, and black pepper and pulse until smooth. Serve at room temperature or chilled. Store in an airtight container in the refrigerator for up to 4 days.

Perfect Vinaigrette

GLUTEN-FREE, GREAT FOR SHABBAT, PAREVE, VEGETARIAN, WEEKEND, WEEKNIGHT

MAKES 1½ CUPS • PREP TIME: 5 MINUTES

This vinaigrette is one of my most versatile recipes ever—it's amazing as a dressing on any salad, but I also frequently use it as a tangy marinade for countless meat dishes (it's especially delicious with oven-roasted chicken breast). Most often, I use it to dress a simple green salad, served as a side to an easy sheet pan recipe, like Crispy Roasted Tofu and Vegetables (page 73) or Sheet Pan Chicken with Root Vegetables and Cabbage (page 91). Needless to say, I always have a batch in my refrigerator.

⅓ cup balsamic vinegar

1 tablespoon honey mustard (I recommend Honeycup brand)

2 garlic cloves, minced

½ teaspoon sea salt

¼ teaspoon freshly ground black pepper

1 tablespoon dried oregano

1 cup olive oil

1. In a medium bowl, combine the vinegar, honey mustard, garlic, salt, pepper, and oregano. Stir until combined.

2. While whisking continuously, drizzle in the olive oil and whisk until the vinaigrette is thick and creamy. Transfer to a 1-pint mason jar. Store in the refrigerator for up to 1 week. Shake before using to reincorporate.

3-Ingredient Olive Dip

GLUTEN-FREE, GREAT FOR SHABBAT, PAREVE, VEGETARIAN,
WEEKEND, WEEKNIGHT

MAKES 2 CUPS (SERVES 4 TO 6) • PREP TIME: 5 MINUTES

This humble but delicious olive dip is one of the easiest recipes I make—and one of my favorites. You can use any type of pitted olive, or a mix. If you want to make this a healthier dip, skip the mayonnaise and use an avocado instead (see Tip). If you do, use green olives for a lovely green hue.

1 (6-ounce) can pitted black olives (or other olives of your choice)

1 cup mayonnaise

¼ teaspoon dried oregano

In a food processor, combine the olives, mayonnaise, and oregano. Pulse until well combined. Serve with bread for dipping. Store in an airtight container in the refrigerator for up to 4 days.

COOKING TIP: If you're using an avocado, be wary of discoloration. Add 1 tablespoon fresh lemon juice to the dip to prevent it from browning quickly, and also prepare the dip just before serving so it maintains its vibrant color.

Shortcut Matbucha
(Tomato and Green Pepper Dip)

GLUTEN-FREE, GREAT FOR SHABBAT, PAREVE,
VEGETARIAN, WEEKEND, WEEKNIGHT

MAKES 2 CUPS (SERVES 4 TO 6) • PREP TIME: 5 MINUTES,
PLUS 30 MINUTES TO COOL / COOK TIME: 20 MINUTES

Matbucha is a dip made with tomatoes and green peppers, originally from the Maghreb (western North Africa) and now extremely popular in Israeli cuisine. I used to get store-bought matbucha every week, so I figured I'd try to make it at home. My version is generally mild, but you could kick it up a notch by adding a tablespoon or two of hot sauce or Israeli Schug (page 125). Serve the matbucha with bread for dipping.

2 tablespoons olive oil

4 garlic cloves, minced

3 (10-ounce) cans diced tomatoes with green chilies (such as Ro-Tel, or see Tip)

1 teaspoon paprika

1 teaspoon sea salt

½ teaspoon freshly ground black pepper

1. In a large, deep skillet, heat the olive oil over medium heat. Once hot, add the garlic and sauté for 1 minute, or until fragrant.

2. Add the diced tomatoes with green chilies and reduce the heat to medium-low. Simmer until all of the liquid has evaporated, about 15 minutes.

3. Stir in the paprika, salt, and pepper. Cook for 1 minute more, or until just fragrant.

4. Let the matbucha cool for at least 30 minutes. Serve at room temperature or refrigerate and serve chilled. Store in an airtight container in the refrigerator for up to 5 days.

INGREDIENT TIP: If you don't have canned diced tomatoes with green chilies, you can substitute 1 (28-ounce) can or 2 (14.5-ounce cans) plain diced tomatoes and half of a 4-ounce can of green chilies (save the other half of the can for another use).

Pareve Caesar Dressing

GLUTEN-FREE, GREAT FOR SHABBAT, PAREVE,
WEEKEND, WEEKNIGHT

MAKES 1¼ CUPS • PREP TIME: 5 MINUTES

Caesar salad is ubiquitous these days at restaurants and in home kitchens alike, but the dressing typically contains dairy, which can be an issue for those of us who keep kosher. And many store-bought pareve Caesar dressings are full of preservatives. This easy, five-ingredient pareve recipe has the creamy taste of traditional Caesar dressing, but you can serve it as part of a meat meal.

1 tablespoon fresh lemon juice

1 tablespoon Pareve Worcestershire sauce

2 garlic cloves, minced

1 teaspoon mustard powder

1 cup mayonnaise

In a medium bowl, stir together the lemon juice, Worcestershire sauce, garlic, and mustard powder. Whisk in the mayonnaise until fully incorporated. Store in an airtight container in the refrigerator for 3 to 4 days.

VARIATION TIP: I leave out the anchovies because my kids prefer this dressing without them, but if you like anchovies, add 1 or 2 finely chopped anchovy fillets to the dressing before mixing. For a gluten-free version, ensure your Worcestershire sauce is gluten-free or use anchovies instead.

Homemade Savory Marinara Sauce

GLUTEN-FREE, GREAT FOR SHABBAT, PAREVE, VEGETARIAN, WEEKEND

MAKES 4 CUPS • PREP TIME: 10 MINUTES / COOK TIME: 1 HOUR

Homemade marinara sauce is simple to make but can elevate pasta, pizza, and so many other dishes to the next level. You'll find this sauce is helpful to have on hand in the refrigerator to whip up a pizza. I sometimes make a double batch and freeze half in ice cube trays, then use the cubes to flavor soups, stews, and other vegetable or meat dishes. Try using in Super-Simple Baked Gefilte Fish (page 67).

2 tablespoons olive oil

1 large onion, finely diced

4 garlic cloves, minced

1 cup red wine

1 (28-ounce) can crushed tomatoes

1 (14-ounce) can whole peeled tomatoes, undrained

1 (8-ounce) can tomato sauce

¼ cup chopped fresh basil

4 scallions, finely chopped

1 teaspoon sea salt

½ teaspoon freshly ground black pepper

1. In a large pot, heat the olive oil over medium heat. Once hot, add the onion and sauté for 5 minutes, or until softened. Add the garlic and sauté for 1 minute more, until fragrant. Add the wine and simmer for 20 minutes to reduce it by half.

2. Stir in the crushed tomatoes, peeled tomatoes and their juices, the tomato sauce, basil, scallions, salt, and pepper. Reduce the heat to low and simmer the sauce for 30 minutes to reduce and thicken.

3. Use an immersion blender to puree the sauce and blend any remaining large chunks (if you prefer a chunky sauce, you can skip this step).

4. Store in an airtight container in the refrigerator for 3 to 4 days. Or freeze in an ice cube tray, then store the cubes in a zip-top bag in the freezer for up to 3 months.

Israeli Schug

MAKES 1½ CUPS • PREP TIME: 20 MINUTES

This spicy, garlicky sauce, which originated in Yemen but is now popular in Israeli cuisine, adds a kick of heat and flavor to almost any dish. A small serving packs a punch, so if you're sensitive to spice, you'll only need a small amount. My husband and kids love spicy food, so we use schug as a topping for chicken, sandwiches, eggs, and so much more. You can freeze extra schug in ice cube trays for easy use—try adding one to Jamie's Shortcut Shakshuka (page 22).

10 garlic cloves, peeled

12 fresh red chile peppers, coarsely chopped

½ cup fresh parsley leaves

Juice of ½ lemon

½ teaspoon ground cumin

½ teaspoon smoked paprika

½ teaspoon freshly ground black pepper

½ teaspoon sea salt

¼ cup olive oil

1. In a food processor, combine the garlic, chiles, parsley, lemon juice, cumin, paprika, black pepper, and salt. Process until finely minced.

2. With the machine running, slowly drizzle in the olive oil and process until the mixture forms a smooth paste.

3. Transfer the schug to a glass jar. Store in the refrigerator for up to 1 week. Or freeze in an ice cube tray, then store the cubes in a zip-top bag in the freezer for up to 3 months.

VARIATION TIP: The above recipe is for a red schug, but green schug is popular as well. For green schug, you can substitute the same amount of jalapeños for the red chiles and use cilantro in place of the parsley.

MEASUREMENT CONVERSIONS

VOLUME EQUIVALENTS (LIQUID)

US STANDARD	US STANDARD (OUNCES)	METRIC (APPROXIMATE)
2 tablespoons	1 fl. oz.	30 mL
¼ cup	2 fl. oz.	60 mL
½ cup	4 fl. oz.	120 mL
1 cup	8 fl. oz.	240 mL
1½ cups	12 fl. oz.	355 mL
2 cups or 1 pint	16 fl. oz.	475 mL
4 cups or 1 quart	32 fl. oz.	1 L
1 gallon	128 fl. oz.	4 L

OVEN TEMPERATURES

FAHRENHEIT (F)	CELSIUS (C) (APPROXIMATE)
250°	120°
300°	150°
325°	165°
350°	180°
375°	190°
400°	200°
425°	220°
450°	230°

VOLUME EQUIVALENTS (DRY)

US STANDARD	METRIC (APPROXIMATE)
⅛ teaspoon	0.5 mL
¼ teaspoon	1 mL
½ teaspoon	2 mL
¾ teaspoon	4 mL
1 teaspoon	5 mL
1 tablespoon	15 mL
¼ cup	59 mL
⅓ cup	79 mL
½ cup	118 mL
⅔ cup	156 mL
¾ cup	177 mL
1 cup	235 mL
2 cups or 1 pint	475 mL
3 cups	700 mL
4 cups or 1 quart	1 L
½ gallon	2 L
1 gallon	4 L

WEIGHT EQUIVALENTS

US STANDARD	METRIC (APPROXIMATE)
½ ounce	15 g
1 ounce	30 g
2 ounces	60 g
4 ounces	115 g
8 ounces	225 g
12 ounces	340 g
16 ounces or 1 pound	455 g

REFERENCES

Emmer, Tzivia, Rivka Katzen, and Tziporah Reitman, eds. *Spice and Spirit: The Complete Kosher Jewish Cookbook.* Lubavitch Women's Cookbook Publications, 1990.

Fishkoff, Sue. *Kosher Nation: Why More and More of America's Food Answers to a Higher Authority.* New York: Schocken Books, 2010.

Scherman, Rabbi Nosson, ed. *The Five Books of the Torah (The Bible): The Stone Edition*, 11th ed. Brooklyn, NY: Mesorah Publications, 2012.

Sohn, Rabbi Ruth H. "The Purpose of Kashrut." My Jewish Learning. Accessed October 7, 2020. myjewishlearning.com/article/the-purpose-of-kashrut.

"Your Kosher Kitchen: A Primer to Going Kosher." OK Kosher Certification. Accessed October 7, 2020. ok.org/consumers/your-kosher-kitchen.

INDEX

Pepper Steak and Vegetables
with Peanut Sauce, 86–87
Roasted Vegetable Soup, 54
Sheet Pan Chicken with Root
Vegetables and Cabbage, 91
Vegetable Ragout Pasta, 74
Vegetarian "Crab" Cakes, 75–77
Vinaigrette, Perfect, 120

W

Walnuts
Not-Your-Ordinary Pesto, 117
Wild Rice and Avocado Salad, 41
Wilted Spinach Salad with
Warm Apples, 45

Y

Yogurt, storing, 13

Z

Za'atar Garlic Hummus, Eggplant
Latkes with, 36–37
Zucchini
Crispy Roasted Tofu and
Vegetables, 73
Zucchini Dill Soup, 57

ACKNOWLEDGMENTS

I would like to thank my loving husband, David, for being my voice of reason and my cheerleader. He has been a steadying influence when my ideas go off-topic or when I try to exceed my reach. He supported me in every way imaginable as I developed my online health, cooking, and nutrition business during the pandemic, a time that made it even more challenging an endeavor. He gives me honest and helpful feedback, and his love and warmth are cherished always. I am so thankful to have him in my life.

I would also like to thank my four daughters—Danielle, Emily, Samantha, and Hannah—for putting up with me while I was writing this book. Even though there were many days that I was working long hours and late in the evening, I still tried to be the best mom possible. I am so thrilled that our COVID-19 quarantine period gave us precious time to cook many exciting meals together. I am so proud of their patience and support and for being my recipe taste testers. I know they will all become great cooks and will follow in my footsteps as well as their grandmothers'. I love you all so much!

I would like to thank my gluten-free family members and friends who are my biggest fans and always tell me how delicious my food is and how they have enjoyed my recipes. And, of course, I would like to thank my mother for always welcoming me in the kitchen and teaching me to cook and enjoy good food.

I hope these recipes provide a little bit of the love in my kitchen to all the readers of this book. Eat well and live better!

ABOUT THE AUTHOR

 **Jamie Feit** is a registered dietitian who teaches busy moms how to prepare healthy gluten-free and kosher food that their families will enjoy, without spending hour upon hour in the kitchen. With a master's degree in clinical nutrition from New York University, Jamie has been helping her patients meet their nutrition goals for more than 20 years.

During her career as a dietitian, Jamie has worked with the prestigious Mount Sinai Medical Center, Blythedale Children's Hospital, and Westmed Medical Group. She now runs a private nutrition and wellness practice in New York and has recently been featured on several podcasts, including *Are We There Yet Moms*, *Are Those Rose Colored Glasses You're Wearing?* (formerly called *Women Are the Journey*), and *Let My People Eat*. Her writing is published in *Thrive Global*, and she is the author of *The Celiac Disease Diet Plan* as well as the creator of the Shabbat Made Easy kosher meal plan program, available on her website at jamiefeitnutrition.com. For more information, contact Jamie at jamie@jamiefeitnutrition.com.

Jamie lives with her husband, their four girls, and a large Bernedoodle in a Modern Orthodox community in Westchester, New York. She keeps a kosher home and loves to entertain friends and family every chance she can get.

CPSIA information can be obtained
at www.ICGtesting.com
Printed in the USA
JSHW010243270421
13897JS00003B/4